REAL WOMEN WRITE

Seeing Through Their Eyes

FOREWORD BY
Marita Golden

EDITED BY
Susan Schoch

**SHARING STORIES, SHARING LIVES
IN PROSE AND POETRY FROM
STORY CIRCLE NETWORK**

A Publication of Story Circle Network

Real Women Write: Seeing Through Their Eyes
Volume 21, 2022

Foreword by Marita Golden
Edited by Susan Schoch
Cover image, interior design, and technical support by Sherry Wachter

Copyright © 2022 by Story Circle Network
Copyrights to all contributed works remain with the authors.

All rights reserved. No part of this book may be reproduced, scanned, or distributed in any printed or electronic form without permission.

ISBN: 978-0-9795329-9-3

Story Circle Network
723 W University Ave #300-234
Georgetown TX 78626

https://www.storycircle.org

Story Circle Network is a nonprofit—501(c)(3)—organization dedicated to helping women share the stories of their lives and to raising public awareness of the importance of women's personal histories. We carry out that mission through publications, websites, classes, workshops, writing and reading circles, and woman-focused programs. SCN activities empower women to tell their stories, discover their identities through their stories, and choose to be the authors of their own lives.

Story Circle Network's 2022 anthology of members' writing, *Real Women Write,* has taken up the topic of empathy, a subject that informs every aspect of our lives today. Contributors explore the impact of *Seeing Through Their Eyes,* including what that encompasses and how all sorts of humans, and also nonhuman species, experience it. Perhaps no action is more important than choosing to learn about and from the perspective of others, and sharing our efforts to do that. This theme speaks to SCN's goal of supporting writing women of all ages, sexual orientations, gender identities, races, religions, and ethnicities.

Empathy is the most mysterious transaction that the
human soul can have, and it's accessible to all of us,
but we have to give ourselves the opportunity to identify,
to plunge ourselves in a story where we see the world
from the bottom up or through another's eyes or heart.

— Sue Monk Kidd

Contents

PG

ix	Foreword	Marita Golden
xiii	Editor's Note	Susan Schoch
xv	About Story Circle Network	Len Leatherwood
xvii	Contributors	

F – Fiction   NF – Nonfiction   P – Poetry

What We Lack

3	Empathy, Reconsidered NF	Lisa Baron
4	Yellowing Curtains P	Lin Brummels
5	Woman Without Empathy NF	Kit Dalton
6	I Want to Thrive NF	Linda Hopkins
9	My Mother and Her Pain NF	Len Leatherwood
11	Sweetheart F	Catherine N. Steinberg
12	Why Did You Say That? NF	Marian McCaa Thomas
14	Talking about Buffalo With the Dead NF	Christina M. Wells
17	Wishes NF	Ariela L. Zucker

Calling Out for Caring

21	Progeny P	Lin Brummels
22	East Young Avenue P	Joan L. Connor
23	Dyscalculia F	B. Lynn Goodwin
24	Lines P	Teresa Lynn
25	I See You NF	Lucy Painter
26	My Mother, the Poet NF	Janet Grace Riehl
28	The Thin Curtain NF	Elena Schwolsky
32	A Poem for Uvalde, Texas P	Madeline Sharples
33	As Thyself F	Monique S. Simón
34	Can I Swim in Your Lane? NF	Catherine N. Steinberg
35	Letter to Our Insolent Server NF	Rhonda Wiley-Jones
38	The Oppressed NF	Charlotte Wlodkowski
40	Mining for Gold or A Tourist Guide to Aging NF	Ariela L. Zucker

STANDING ALONE

47	Interview NF	Kathie Arcide
48	To the Mothers of Uvalde NF	Sharon L. Charde
51	Generational Trauma NF	Debra Dolan
54	This Too Shall Pass NF	Carolyn Foland
56	I'm Afraid P	Juliana Lightle
57	Short Talk with Dorothy on Her Birthday P	Margaret Dubay Mikus
58	Self-Empathy, Healthy Compassion, and Trees NF	Sandra Stanko
62	Veterans Day at the Veterans Memorial P	Pamela Stockwell
63	Cracks That Need Healing P	Jo Virgil
64	Through Her Eyes P	Ariela L. Zucker

EXPLORING THE MYSTERY

66	Ancestry Surprise NF	Patricia Daly
69	Rethinking Marriage F	Kathryn Haueisen
72	My Son's Eyes NF	Christy-Holly Piszkiewicz
73	Two Rivers Flowing NF	Janet Grace Riehl
75	Truth or Lie NF	Marlene B. Samuels
77	Just in Time NF	Elena Schwolsky
81	Through My Mother's Eyes NF	Connie Spittler
84	My Husband Died Twice NF	Marian McCaa Thomas
86	Paying to Pee NF	Rhonda Wiley-Jones

LESSONS LEARNED

93	Lessons on Racism from a Remote Island in Fiji NF	Kathie Arcide
96	Rewrite the Sign NF	Claire Butler
98	Field of Dreams NF	Sara Etgen-Baker
101	Will Work for Food NF	Linda Healy
104	Communal Ties NF	Shawn Marie LaTorre
106	Soaking Up Early Lessons on Ecology NF	Melanie McGauran
109	The Gifts of Fiction P	Margaret Dubay Mikus
110	Lesson Learned in a Bathroom Stall NF	Erin Philbin
111	Empathy is Emotional Mindfulness P	Sandra Stanko
112	KJ The Empathetic Cat NF	Marian McCaa Thomas

GIVING AND RECEIVING

117	Five Women Around a Table NF	Sharon L. Charde
120	Make It Matter that It Did NF	Christine Hassing
124	Love Blooms in Costco NF	Jane Gragg Lewis
125	Empathy: The Ripple Effect NF	Julie Ryan McGue
129	Empathetic Laughing Eyes NF	Christy-Holly Piszkiewicz
131	Hershey, The Man NF	Marlene B. Samuels
135	Sun Sets on a Sufi P	Monique S. Simón
136	Empathy in the Time of COVID NF	Jo-Ann Vega
139	Just Thirty Seconds NF	Jude Walsh
140	Sauerkraut, Pecan Pies, and Tanning Beds NF	Christina M. Wells

HOW IT COULD BE

147	Married to the U.S. Disabled Ski Team – Three Moments of Perspective NF	Kathie Arcide
151	You're Special – Words of Empathy NF	Carol J. Wechsler Blatter
154	Daily Life in Our Digital Age NF	Cynthia F. Davidson
157	The Poor Little Matchstick Girl NF	Sara Etgen-Baker
160	Your Reputation Ain't Ruined, Honey F	B. Lynn Goodwin
160	The Power of Empathy NF	Patricia Roop Hollinger
163	What Do You Need? P	Len Leatherwood
164	The Bridge to Understanding P	Juliana Lightle
164	I Will Take You Halfway NF	Janet Grace Riehl
167	I Am Called P	Catherine N. Steinberg
168	An Angel With No Wings NF	Jo Virgil
169	Understood NF	Jude Walsh
172	How to Save Your Life F	Linda C. Wisniewski
176	I Live In A Boy's Body F	Margie Witt

FOREWORD
Marita Golden

The essays in this anthology explore the myriad ways that we wrestle with the requirements of empathy, how difficult empathy is to express, and how wondrous it feels to submit to its invitation. These narratives are diverse and surprising and take us from a writing workshop for women struggling to overcome addiction and the walled off cities and hearts of the Middle East, to the world of social media seen as a thread allowing us to literally reach out and almost touch somebody's life, if not their hand.

The definition of empathy is elegant in its clarity and simplicity: *The ability to understand and share the feelings of others.* If empathy is defined as an ability, then that means it is a skill, perhaps even a talent. If it is a skill or a talent, then empathy can be learned, acquired. Clearly, empathy is a form of love. *Love* — that most loaded, feared, and challenging of four-letter words. Empathy allows us to be guided by our hearts and to absorb the pain and injuries of others, in a sense to take that pain and injury onto ourselves. To carry the full weight of relationship.

When we say that we have been deeply moved by a narrative, we are acknowledging that the writer mastered the art of empathy. The writer has convinced us as readers that they fully understand the subject, and that they entered without hesitation the lives of the people in the narrative. They understand, and understanding trumps judgment. Empathy is necessary for complex, dimensional observation and writing.

The wisdom and compassion of these narratives is a gift for writer and reader. I keep gratefully recalling these words from the essays:

> "…listening with her trained ear to their pain and their isolation…. Who knows the pain that lurks under the surface? … We all best be kind-hearted."
> — from *My Mother and Her Pain*

> "Walls create a physical divide, but people do the rest."
> — from *Wishes*

> "Seren, you've changed my life forever. I'll never forget you!"
> "And Hershey, you saved my life. I'll always remember you."
> — from *Hershey, The Man*

"'Write about that,' I said. 'Just write about anything. You can do it.' And slowly, she did. She read with all of us, hesitantly at first, and then came out of the shadows to really join in. … We are all so human together."
— from *Five Women Around a Table*

"They can't see who I am. With a tender touch she reaches for my hand…."
— from *I Live in a Boy's Body*

In our collective rearview mirror, we see the outline of pandemic, lockdown, quarantine on a global scale. We learned how connected we are, how interdependent we are. We created new forms of communication and intimacy. Our empathy was stretched thin. And yet out of all that, we learned how fragile we are and how necessary we are for one another.

My writing has blessed me over and over. I awaken from the slumber of complacency each time I strive to write a beautiful sentence, an endeavor that requires time and a deep investment of heart and soul. A beautiful sentence provides insight, and inspires awe at what language can accomplish, how it can even change the direction of one's life and dreams. My writing is where I strive to be my best self. Principled but not dogmatic. Building bridges by revealing and discovering shared fragility and vulnerability. Seeing not only my face in the mirror but also the faces of others. Embracing the belief that the truth is multicolored, multicultural, multiracial, relative, divisive, unifying. And the truth, confounding as it is, can set us free.

Now as much as at any other time in human history, we need to tell ourselves and others stories grounded in empathy and compassion. There is the swing toward authoritarianism. The growing intolerance of differing views. The push to make the toxic ideology of White Supremacy respectable as an impulse and movement. The insidious dangers of social media and technology. These are all tangible, real pressures targeting community. These are pressures that make any story that is not embedded in empathy irrelevant and dangerous.

As the definition of "story," what it is and why it is important, seems to shift into unrecognizable territory, we must tell our children and grandchildren our stories. They need to know where we have been, what we have survived, and what we know that they can use to build tomorrow.

The narratives in this collection dive into the deep end of the pool, where the water is wide and deep and where you discover what you are made of. What you can do. These essays urge you to turn away from your cell phone, television, or computer screen, to hear the real breaking news — that we are in this life and in this world together. We *must* love one another. These narratives show how we *can* love one another.

Marita Golden is the award-winning author of twenty works of fiction and nonfiction, most recently *The Strong Black Woman: How a Myth Endangers the Physical and Mental Health of Black Women.* https://maritagolden.com

Editor's Note
Susan Schoch

Seeing Through Their Eyes is Volume 21 in SCN's annual members' anthology, *Real Women Write*.

In our 2021 edition, *Beyond COVID: Leaning Into Tomorrow*, we looked to the future post-pandemic. In 2022, the reality of that persistent virus has become clear. We're adapting to the ongoing threat. But we've also turned our attention to other dangers, such as climate change and its related disasters, war in Ukraine leading to increased global famine, economic fall-out from COVID and corporate greed, and escalating gun violence. We are nearly numb to disasters.

Yet we're learning, too, about what humans can do to make things better. As we consider how to make a difference, so that we <u>don't</u> grow numb and we continue to take care of each other and the planet, developing the quality of *empathy* is vital. It naturally became the theme of this 2022 volume, and the idea of empathy inspired a wide range of stories and poems in our contributors. In these 75 works by 49 writers, you will surely find responses that speak to you.

As Marita Golden says in her Foreword to this collection, "These essays urge you to turn away from your cell phone, television, or computer screen, to hear the real breaking news — that we are in this life and in this world together." Some of the authors here tell of times when they were suffering and longed for the understanding of others. Some tell about moments when they were able to offer that compassion to those in need. Some admit their failures to see another's reality. And some find themselves opening their minds and hearts to strangers.

More than ever, SCN understands the value of diversity, and we celebrate that in *Real Women Write* with a readable chorus of our members' voices, creating unanticipated harmony. Because we appreciate the individual, editing here is light, and coherence comes from the subject, rather than from consistency of style. Of course, simple errors that might cause confusion or impede reading, like misplaced commas, misspellings, shifts in tense or incorrect grammar, have been corrected.

While the anthology includes a generous sampling of entries received, selection is limited. We work hard to choose the best writing—relevant, engaging, worth your time—and also publish writers of varied experience and opportunity.

Editing *Real Women Write* is always a rewarding and growthful experience, and I am grateful for the extraordinary women of Story Circle Network, who work with me to create this annual member showcase. Among them are Susan Wittig Albert, founder of SCN, mentor and steadfast advisor; Len Leatherwood, president of SCN, provider of good counsel and vital support; Teresa Lynn, vital technical manager of submission processes and website pages; Liz Beaty, who keeps finances and program goals in sight; the Board of Directors, who continue to support this member opportunity; Sherry Wachter, for superlative cover art, book design, and technical formatting; and our Publications Chair, Shelley Carey, who guards the vision for SCN books and authors.

We all have great appreciation for the thoughtful contribution of Marita Golden, author of our Foreword. Her timely and important writing continues to inform and inspire many women.

And all of us are thankful to the SCN members who submitted their works for this unique issue. Their creativity and insightful writing will have impact for years to come, and make a significant contribution to the herstory of our time.

About Story Circle Network: Dedicated to "Seeing Through Their Eyes"

Len Leatherwood

> Empathy is really the opposite of spiritual meanness.
> It's the capacity to understand that every war is both won
> and lost. And that someone else's pain is as
> meaningful as your own.
>
> — Barbara Kingsolver

As president of Story Circle Network, I am delighted that our organization has published a book that focuses on empathy. There is no better way to celebrate our 25th Anniversary and to illustrate the founding principles that New York Times bestselling author Susan Wittig Albert had in mind when she established SCN back in 1997. SCN's mission is to honor women's histories and to celebrate their stories, large and small. The purpose of that mission is to not only give women a stronger voice, but also to help build a more empathetic world.

Our organization offers a wide range of opportunities and programs to help fulfill that mission. We provide women with online and in-person classes, monthly webinars, national and international writing workshops, a yearly virtual writing conference, virtual reading and writing circles, publication opportunities, and writing competitions. We also hope soon to resume our biennial in-person writing conference.

In addition, we sponsor Story Circle Book Reviews, the largest and oldest women's book review site on the Internet, as well as the annual Sarton Women's Writing Awards and the Gilda Awards. Moreover, we are committed to diversity and inclusion, and are actively working to add more BIPOC, LGBTQ+ women, and women with disabilities to our ranks. This past year we also became partners with College Match to mentor economically disadvantaged high school girls. We want to encourage *all* women to tell their stories.

We provide our members with a variety of ways to publish their lifewriting, memoir, poetry, fiction and nonfiction. Not only do we have two blogs, "Telling HerStories" and "One Woman's Day," but we also publish the quarterly "Story Circle Journal" and have published more than twenty annual *Real Women Write* anthologies. In addition, SCN has published five collections of members' and others' writing: *With Courage and Common Sense: Memoirs from the Older Women's Legacy Circle; What Wildness is This: Women Write about the Southwest; Kitchen Table Stories 2007* and *2022;* and *Inside and Out.*

In the past 25 years, SCN has touched the lives of over 4000 members from the U.S. and other countries. As a nonprofit, we operate with a small paid staff and a large contingent of dedicated volunteers. Our funding comes from annual membership dues, program fees, and generous donations from grants and supporters.

We welcome writers at all levels, from novice to expert, and encourage all forms of writing. We are eager to provide guidance, support, and camaraderie to any woman who wants to add her voice to the chorus of women who count Story Circle Network as a safe haven to share their stories with one another as well as with the world.

Please visit our website at https://www.storycircle.org/.

Len Leatherwood is the current president of Story Circle Network. Please see her bio in the Contributors section.

Contributors

Kathie Arcide – Bellevue WA
Kathie Arcide is Mom, Gramma, and Psychotherapist in private practice for 45 years. But more important, I am my father's daughter. My calling is to pass on his creative, and often covert, childhood lessons to his daughters, the most valuable one being the ability we all have to choose how we see or experience a person, place or thing. Seeing through others' eyes is my lifelong mission. My blog is https://chosenperspectives.com/

Lisa Baron – Pittsboro NC
Dr. Lisa Baron is a writer, teacher, therapist, and mentor. She has filled journals with poetry and reflections for many years. Her writing reflects her strong commitment to introspection, and has been published in Story Circle's *Beyond COVID: Leaning Into Tomorrow* anthology, The New Social Worker, and Natural Awakenings. She is in the process of co-authoring a book with two other women writers on the conversations we have with our younger selves. Her website is lisabaroncreative.com.

Carol J. Wechsler Blatter – Tucson AZ
Mrs. Blatter is a recently retired psychotherapist. She has published stories in Chaleur Press, Jewish Writing Project, *Writing It Real* anthologies, prose poems in Story Circle Network's *Real Women Write* anthologies, in *Covenant of the Generations* by the Women of Reform Judaism, and stories on 101words.org. Mrs. Blatter is a wife, mother, and grandmother. She is ecstatic when she listens to her eight-year-old granddaughter read her creative storybook writings.

Lin Brummels – Winside NE
Lin Marshall Brummels earned a Psychology B.A. from the University of Nebraska and an M.S. in Rehabilitation Counseling from Syracuse University. She's a Nebraska licensed mental health counselor. Brummels has published poems in journals, magazines, and anthologies, and served as Poetry Out Loud judge at Northeast Nebraska's Regional Semi-Finals. Her poetry chapbooks are "Cottonwood Strong" and "Hard Times," a 2016 Nebraska Book Award winner. Her book of poems, *A Quilted Landscape*, was published in 2021.

Claire Butler – Cincinnati OH
I hail from Cincinnati, and have published one book, *Conversations With the Tuesday Night Girls*, and written a memoir that is finished and edited, waiting for revision. I've been published in three anthologies, many short-story sites, one magazine and a newspaper. I am also a professional artist, working in oil on canvas, and my workspace/studio is in my home, where my fur baby Tilly lies at my feet whether I am writing or painting. Claire-Butler.com

Sharon L. Charde – Lakeville CT
I have seven published collections of poetry, and a memoir, *I Am Not A Juvenile Delinquent*, about my sixteen years of volunteer-teaching poetry to delinquent girls, how it changed both them and me (Mango Publishing, June 2020). The BBC adapted my full-length collection, *Branch In His Hand*, as an hour-long radio drama, which was broadcast in 2012. I have seven Pushcart nominations, have won many awards and residency fellowships including MacDowell and Yaddo, and have been published over 85 times in journals and anthologies.

Joan L. Connor – Kerrville TX
Joan lives in Kerrville, Texas, and also in her travel trailer, as she, Husband, and Dog Ava spend summers in the Pacific Northwest. She is completing a Peace Corps memoir (Mongolia 2011-2013), part of which constituted her thesis for a recently acquired M.F.A. from Lindenwood University. Currently, she is on track to become a certified journal facilitator. When not tapping the computer keys, Joan spends hours as a novice fiddler, lifelong pianist, neophyte painter, and bicycling along the Guadalupe River.

Kit Dalton – Walnut Creek CA
I live in senior housing in Walnut Creek, California. I find the location very agreeable, and my two cats are getting to like it better. I retired in 2008 from teaching English Composition and ESL to community college and adult school students. While teaching, I contributed ESL sections to two English Composition textbooks. After retiring, I began a memoir of my experience of WWII in Hawaii and in the U.S. It is now complete and in search of a publisher.

Patricia Daly – Largo FL
Patricia Daly is a USA Today bestselling author and writer of narrative nonfiction and spirituality. She has been published by Leaders Press,

Story Circle Network, *The Sun*, and *Reiki News Magazine*. She has indie-published *The Women in His Life* and *Indelible Imprint*, both available on Amazon. Her new book, *The Deliberate Thinker*, was published in October 2021. She is retired and lives in Largo, Florida. Connect with her at www.PatriciaDalyWrites.com.

Cynthia F. Davidson – Hope Valley RI
A member of SCN for over a dozen years, Cynthia F. Davidson is now a member of the board and on the faculty. A long time expatriate and former CBS News journalist, she spent two decades as a pioneer in the global management field. She credits SCN membership with the support and skill development required to publish her first memoir, *The Importance of Paris*. SCN also inspired her to start facilitating workshops and writing groups that capture women's lived wisdom. https://cynthiafdavidson.com

Debra Dolan – West Vancouver BC Canada
Debra Dolan lives on the west coast of Canada, is a long time (50+ years) private journal writer, and an avid reader of women's memoir. She has been a member of Story Circle Network since 2009 and is a self-described pluviophile. Debra enjoys deep conversations over red wine and candlelight, solo nature walks, and has completed two book projects, *Writings and Reflections: 1958 to 2018* and *Writings and Reflections: Turning 50 in 2008, Walking the Camino de Santiago*.

Sara Etgen-Baker – Anna TX
A teacher's unexpected whisper, "You've got writing talent," ignited Sara's writing desire. She ignored that whisper and pursued a different career but eventually rediscovered her inner writer. Sara has written over 150 memoir vignettes, many of which have been published in anthologies and magazines, including *Good Old Days Magazine, Chicken Soup for the Soul, Guideposts, Times They Were A-Changing,* and *Wisdom Has a Voice*. She recently finished writing her first novel, *Secrets at Dillehay Crossing*.

Carolyn Foland – Sacramento CA
At 78, I am retired from work in the health and welfare field. With degrees in both journalism and public administration, I created public information and education programs in mental health, and later worked in program monitoring, contract development, and facility management. I enjoy travel, writing, reading, and cultural events including plays and lectures. I have two cats, Faith and Hope, who permit me to live with them if I maintain certain standards relating to their care.

B. Lynn Goodwin – Danville CA
Writer and editor B. Lynn Goodwin owns Writer Advice, www.writeradvice.com. She's the author of two award-winning books, a Young Adult novel called *Talent* and a memoir titled *Never Too Late: From Wannabe to Wife at 62*, plus an out-of-print self-help book. Her flash fiction is published in *Flashquake, Nebo, The Cabinet of Heed, Murmur of Words, 100-Word Stories, Ariel's Dream*, and *Writing in a Woman's Voice*. Her second YA, *Disrupted*, is forthcoming. She's also a reviewer and teacher at Story Circle Network.

Christine Hassing – Bloomingdale MI
Life Story writer/teacher, author, life coach, advocate of cold noses as healers and champion of unconditional listening and hope, Christine Hassing has published two life-story books (her personal memoir *To the Moon and Back to Me: What I Learned from Four Running Feet* and *Hope Has a Cold Nose*, a collection of twenty-three military veteran life stories). Christine resides with her husband and two cold noses in fur, where her noisiest neighbors are bullfrogs.

Kathryn Haueisen – Houston TX
My books cover the challenges of moving, recovering from a natural disaster, tips for journaling and reflections, adjusting to the single-again life after a divorce, and what really brought the Pilgrims to this continent. I blog regularly to promote good people doing great things and publish articles and books when I can. Published books: *Married & Mobile; A Ready Hope; 40-Day Journey with Kathleen Norris; Asunder;* and *Mayflower Chronicles: The Tale of Two Cultures*. My website: HowWiseThen.com

Linda Healy – Kettering OH
Linda Healy was a hospice nurse in her career. She now writes legacy pieces and poetry. She also enjoys color pencil drawing and Zentangles. Other activities include hiking, pets, travel, movies and books. Her favorite pastime is spending time with her grandchildren.

Patricia Roop Hollinger – Westminster MD
"Pat" was raised on a farm, thus developed an imagination pondering the nature of the universe as plants emerged from seeds the size of a grain of salt. Words held the magic of stories. She sings words to her own accompaniment on the piano or organ. She is a retired Chaplain/Pastoral Counselor/Licensed Clinical Professional Counselor, who lives in a retirement community with her husband and their cat, "Spunky."

Linda Hopkins – Portland OR
Linda Hopkins opened the Healing Earth Center in 2020. She loves to garden and is a facilitator of the Work That Reconnects. She lives in Portland, Oregon, with her husband and two teenage children. https://healingearthcenter.com/

Shawn Marie LaTorre – Austin TX
Shawn, a star book reviewer for Story Circle Network and a member of a local Story Circle book group, retired from secondary education years ago. She now spends summers sailing the Great Lakes aboard HMS Juicy Fruit and the other nine months in Austin mentoring, volunteering, quilting, and spinning tales. You can visit her blog at CeruleanSeasons.com or follow her educational tweets as MizLaTee on Twitter, or see some of her quilts on Facebook.

Len Leatherwood – Beverly Hills CA
Len Leatherwood, the current president of Story Circle Network and the Program Coordinator for SCN's Online Classes program, has been teaching writing privately to students in Beverly Hills for the past 22 years. She is a nationally recognized writing coach as well as an award-winning author. Len has published work in flash fiction and nonfiction and has been nominated for a Pushcart Prize. Her blog, "20 Minutes a Day," can be found at lenleatherwood.com.

Jane Gragg Lewis – Laguna Niguel CA
Jane Gragg Lewis lives in Southern California, where she enjoys the near-perfect weather riding her bike, playing Pickleball, kayaking, visiting or volunteering at the San Diego Zoo/Safari Park. She has published two books, *Dictation Riddles* (an ESL activity text) and a memoir, *A Jar of Fireflies*.

Juliana Lightle – San Dimas CA
The author of books, poems, and articles, Juliana Lightle moved from Texas to California in the summer of 2021. A longtime member of SCN, she has served on the board, attended conferences and taken courses, and is currently working on a chapbook of feminist poetry. She has worked for two large corporations, two universities, raised and trained racehorses, and taught high school. Her latest book, *You're Gonna Eat That?!* features stories and food from the all over the world.

Teresa Lynn – Georgetown TX
Teresa Lynn is a writer and editor, who has written for a range of publications on a variety of topics. In addition to writing, she provides all types of editorial and book design services. In her free time, Teresa enjoys reading, traveling, and seeking out little-known history of interesting people and places. She lives in Georgetown with her husband, near their two grown daughters. Reach her through her blog at: https://www.teresalynneditor.com/.

Melanie McGauran – Viera FL
Melanie McGauran started freelance writing in suburban Chicago, covering topics like cloning, heart disease, and her "Day in the Life" series. She also worked at Legacy.com, where they manage newspaper obituaries around the world. After moving to Florida's Space Coast, she continued to volunteer in trash pick-up efforts. She enjoys finding sea turtle nests. Three years ago, Melanie started a blog focusing on her aging mother and nonfiction feature stories. She's a recent cancer survivor.

Julie Ryan McGue – Sarasota FL
Julie Ryan McGue is an American writer. Her award-winning memoir, *Twice a Daughter: A Search for Identity, Family, and Belonging* was released in May 2021. On her weekly blog, "That Girl This Life," Julie writes about finding out who you are, where you come from, and making sense of it. Her work has appeared in the *Story Circle Journal, Brevity, Imprint, Adoption.com, Lifetime Adoption, Adoption & Beyond*, and *Severance Magazine*. She is currently working on a second memoir.

Margaret Dubay Mikus – Lake Forest IL
Margaret Dubay Mikus has published five poetry collections, including *Thrown Again into the Frazzle Machine*. Her CD, *Full Blooming*, has 56 selected short poems and 3 original songs. She also created a personal writing guide using her popular poem, "I Am Willing." Margaret was the 2013 Illinois Featured Author for the *Willow Review*. Her poems, photographs, and essays have frequently appeared online and in print, and her blog at www.FullBlooming.com includes 67 poem-videos.

Lucy Painter – Willow Street PA
I live just outside Lancaster, Pennsylvania, where my husband and I retired to live closer to family. I write every day that I can, and am working on poetry and flash fiction, both a challenge for me.

Erin Philbin – Pittsburgh PA
Erin Philbin is married to Christopher Boyle and has two children. She loves reading, writing, and all manner of fiber crafts. She also loves silliness and adventures with friends.

Christy-Holly Piszkiewicz – Spring Valley OH
Christy Piszkiewicz grew up in Chicago and raised her three children in its suburb of Des Plaines. Moving to Ohio (2014) to be near her two grandchildren, she and her husband, Paul, now reside on a "Hobby Farm." Being a Beekeeper, she enjoys making fruit jams (some fresh-picked!) and exploring nature. Storytelling, writing down and making up stories with her grandkids, is her passion. Sharing her love for God, she has taught parish religious education for more than forty years.

Janet Grace Riehl – Godfrey IL
Artist and writer Janet Riehl is the author of the award-winning book *Sightlines: A Poet's Diary* and the subsequent audio book *Sightlines: A Family Love Story in Poetry and Music*—memoirs told in story-poems. Her poems, stories, and essays have been published in national literary magazines and anthologies. You can find her work online at "Riehlife: Village Wisdom for the 21st Century" (www.riehlife.com) where her mission is to create connections through the arts and across cultures.

Marlene B. Samuels – Chicago IL
Marlene Samuels is an author, research sociologist, instructor and lecturer. When not writing about sociology, her passions include creative nonfiction, flash-nonfiction, photography, and her Rhodesian Ridgebacks, Ted and George. Marlene earned her Ph.D. from University of Chicago, where she serves on the Graduate School Advisory Council. Her books include: *The Seamstress: A Memoir of Survival* and *When Digital Isn't Real: Fact-finding Off Line for Serious Writers*. Her new memoir is forthcoming at the end of 2022.

Elena Schwolsky – Brooklyn NY
Elena Schwolsky is a retired nurse who lives and writes in Brooklyn, New York. Her published works include *Waking in Havana: A Memoir of AIDS and Healing in Cuba* and essays in "The American Journal of Nursing," "Intima: A Journal of Narrative Medicine," and the anthologies *Reflections on Nursing: 80 inspiring stories on the art and science of nursing; The Healer's Burden: Stories and Poems of Professional Grief;* and *Real Women Write: Living on COVID Time*. www.elenaschwolsky.com

Madeline Sharples – Playa Vista CA
Madeline Sharples authored *Papa's Shoes: A Polish shoemaker and his family settle in small-town America* (historical fiction); a memoir in prose and poetry, *Leaving the Hall Light On: A Mother's Memoir of Living with Her Son's Bipolar Disorder and Surviving His Suicide*; and *Blue-Collar Women: Trailblazing Women Take on Men-Only Jobs*. She co-edited *The Great American Poetry Show* anthology and wrote the poems for *The Emerging Goddess* photograph book. Her poems have appeared online and in print.

Monique S. Simón – Binghamton NY
Born in Antigua in the Caribbean, and raised between St. Thomas (USVI) and Antigua, Ms. Simón is an award-winning writer of fiction, creative nonfiction, and poetry. After the life-altering diagnosis of *Myalgic Encephalomyelitis/Chronic Fatigue Syndrome* (ME/CFS), she was compelled to retire from life as a college professor and educational programs developer. With many adjustments to her sense of active time and down time, she has returned to her life as a writer, with a bit more humor and a lot more faith. https://www.facebook.com/Monique-Susanna-Simon-137525539651375/

Connie Spittler – Omaha NE
Connie Spittler writes in several genres. As author/editor, her most recent book, *Turkey Creek Preserve: A Sacred Journey*, is in final proofing before publication. A coffee-table book with over 200 color photographs of birds, mammals, insects and arachnids, other wild creatures, plants, trees, lakes, marshes, wetlands and creeks from seven nature photographers, it's the story of 900 acres of farmland reverting back to Nebraska prairie as natural habitat.

Sandra Stanko – Kittanning PA
Sandra Stanko is a nonfiction, personal growth writer. Beginning her career in corporate communications, she currently works in post-secondary education and lifelong learning. Sandra specializes in journaling applications in the areas of nature writing, spirituality, and writer development. She is pursuing certification as a Pennsylvania Master Naturalist, and as a Certified Journal Facilitator through the Therapeutic Writing Institute. She holds a Ph.D. in composition studies. www.sandrastanko.com

Catherine N. Steinberg – Guilford CT
I am a licensed marriage and family therapist and have been practicing psychotherapy for over forty years. I am also a shamanic practitioner, artist, and workshop/retreat facilitator. Combining my skills and talents, I have developed a meditative approach to painting that I use as well as teach to others. Since my husband died in 2021, my interest in creative writing has reawakened and I am on the second draft of my memoir and also writing flash fiction.

Pamela Stockwell – Manalapan NJ
Pamela Stockwell lives with her husband and three children on a small farm in New Jersey. Her first novel, *A Boundless Place*, won the 2020 LBW Page 100 Writing Competition and is a finalist in the FAPA Annual President's Book Awards Contest. Her poetry has appeared in "Sparked Literary Magazine" and *Hope: An Anthology of Hopeful Stories and Poetry* by TL;DR Press.

Marian McCaa Thomas – Leawood KS
I am a keyboard musician (harpsichord, organ and piano) and consider myself a medial woman. (See Toni Wolff's writing!) I enjoy reading and writing, gardening, maintaining old friendships and making new friends. I try to help combat climate change (solar panels on our house!) and work for peace and justice. The biography I wrote about my mother, *Make Love Your Aim,* has been published! I am adjusting to life without my husband of nearly 59 years. Writing helps!

Jo-Ann Vega – Millsboro DE
I am a published author and dynamic speaker with 30 years of experience presenting to academic, business, and community groups. Recent works include *Moments in Flight: A Memoir* and a forthcoming book of poetry, *Wolf Woman & Other Poems*. A devotee of journaling, I live with my life partner and a canine companion.

Jo Virgil – Austin TX
Jo Virgil lives in Austin, Texas, and retired from a career in journalism and community relations. She has a Master of Journalism degree with a minor in Environmental Science, reflecting her love of writing and appreciation of nature, and has had stories and poetry published in various books, newspapers, and magazines, including Story Circle Network's publications. She lives by words she learned from one of her journalism professors: "Stories are what make us matter."

Jude Walsh – Dayton OH
Jude Walsh writes personal essays, self-help, and romance. As a Creativity and Life Coach and the author of *Post-Divorce Bliss: Ending Us and Finding Me*, she helps women find their superpowers and create a life to match. She is published in numerous anthologies and literary magazines. A Story Circle member since 2005 and a current board member, she credits SCN with lighting the spark that inspired her to become a full-time writer. www.secondbloomcoaching.com and www.judewalsh.com

Christina M. Wells – Annandale VA
Christina M. Wells is an editor and coach who lives in Northern Virginia. She has published in the *SCN Journal*, *Northern Virginia Review*, *Crab Fat Magazine*, *bioStories*, *Big Muddy*, and *Sinister Wisdom*, among others. She is also in *Hashtag Queer Volume 3*, *Is It Hot in Here, or is it Just Me?*, and *Real Women Write: Living on COVID Time*. She has an M.A. from University of Arkansas and a Ph.D. from University of Maryland. Find her online at bychristinamwells.net.

Rhonda Wiley-Jones – Kerrville TX
Rhonda Wiley-Jones taught the SCN classes "Travel Touchstones," and "Learning from the Best Women Travel Writers," and other travel journal writing, travel writing, and the craft of writing for community members, college faculty, and students face-to-face. Wiley-Jones' travel memoir is *At Home in the World: Travel Stories of Growing Up and Growing Away*. Her short stories, essays, and travel memoirs are published online and in anthologies. Her debut novel, *Song of Herself*, will be on bookshelves in early fall 2022.

Linda C. Wisniewski – Doylestown PA
Linda C. Wisniewski is a former librarian who lives with her retired scientist husband and their rescue cat, Denyse, in Doylestown, Pennsylvania. She has been a feature writer for two local newspapers, and teaches memoir workshops and volunteers at the historic home of author Pearl S. Buck. Linda is the author of a memoir, *Off Kilter: A Woman's Journey to Peace with Scoliosis, Her Mother and Her Polish Heritage*, and a time-travel novel, *Where the Stork Flies*.

Margie Witt – Lafayette CA
Margie has been a member of Story Circle Network for over two decades and has participated in writing circles, occasionally contributed to the Journal, and attended two national conferences. Her memoir remains unpublished at the request of her family. She often posts lighthearted #hermanandmyrtle 50-word stories as @mzbull on Instagram. She claims these snippets are fiction but often they are inspired by the happenings of life. https://www.wittbits.com

Charlotte Wlodskowski – Pittsburgh PA
Writing family stories was the beginning of recognizing a new form of communication for me—writing. Last year, I self-published my first book, titled, *Little Bits of This and That with Stories In Between*. It includes Inspirational Essays, Whimsical Readings, Observations from Life, and Fiction and Nonfiction Stories. Hopefully it will give women courage and determination to live their own life.

Ariela L. Zucker – Ellsworth ME
Ariela Zucker was born in Israel. She and her husband left twenty years ago and now reside in Ellsworth, Maine, where they run a Mom-and-Pop motel. Ariela writes poetry and nonfiction, offers online classes, and blogs regularly at Paper Dragon. https://paperdragonme.wordpress.com/

Edited by Susan Schoch, a Colorado freelance writer and editor specializing in personal history. She is author of *The Clay Connection*, a biography of renowned ceramic artists Jim and Nan McKinnell, for the American Museum of Ceramic Art. She also reviews books by and about women at Story Circle Book Reviews, and edited the 2017 essay collection, *Inside and Out*, as well as the recipe/story collection, *Kitchen Table Stories 2022*. Since 2014, she has been editor of SCN's annual *Real Women Write* anthology series.

WHAT WE LACK

Empathy, Reconsidered
Lisa Baron

My father used to say that he knew "exactly" what I felt. Though I am certain that his intentions were pure, that phrase never sat well with me.

He was a man with a big heart, who wanted to shield his people from the bumps of living. Yet, the truth is we can never understand "exactly" how another person feels. There is always a space between our own experiences and another's.

This is particularly challenging when it comes to someone we love. We want to soothe, eradicate, or fix any hurt that they might experience. We want to wave a wand to make it all better—quickly, efficiently, and seamlessly. As painful as it is to watch others go through dark and challenging times, it is part of being alive.

In the past few years, our world has raged with a variety of pandemics, including COVID, as well as racial and economic inequality. We watch news reports in horror as gun violence, unfair treatment of people all over the world, and more, flash on screens, repeatedly reminding us of the fractured world we live in.

We can think of ourselves as empathic, but it's impossible to completely empathize with a parent who has lost a child, a person who lives with a chronic and debilitating disease, or a community that continues to be marginalized. Proposing to understand the complexity of another's emotions and experiences diminishes the reality that we are all separate in our own right.

The best we can do is to look in the mirror at our own attitudes, beliefs, and judgments—and consider ourselves an ongoing "work in progress." We can offer our support by asking a person or a community what we can best do to ease the pain. We can listen, truly listen, offering a helping hand or heart while trying to widen our perspective.

We live in a time where the need for compassion is key, love and forgiveness and open-mindedness are essential. Instead of proposing to match the emotion of another's experience, let us begin by seriously looking inward, where change begins.

Yellowing Curtains
Lin Brummels

Dad stands in our tiny kitchen,
his five-foot-eight-inches slumped
and tired, back to the blazing cob burner
warming his bones. He's already
in cap and ripped jacket,
dust pooling around his overshoes,
sipping one last cup of coffee
before morning chores.
He places the empty cup
on the enameled range behind
the cob stove, turns to leave when
Mom wraps her arms around his neck
to hug him. His now empty arms
hang limp at his sides, eyes
looking away and over her shoulder
toward the once-pretty yellow curtains
tucked behind the water heater.
Suddenly, no longer hungry
for my bowl of Grapenuts,
I look away too, not wanting
to see my mother's face.

WOMAN WITHOUT EMPATHY
Kit Dalton

I absolutely should not have accepted the invitation. Weekday evenings had never been optimal for dinner parties, especially ones with strangers. Most especially for a person with a post-cold sinus infection. But I'd let my husband persuade me, saying the hosts were interesting, agreeable people, both university professors, the wife Swedish, which would normally have been a big draw for me, being fluent in the language and familiar with the culture.

So I patched myself together, and crossed my fingers that the couple would surely understand my fragile state of health if I explained briefly, and would—accordingly—keep things low-key. But no such luck.

We were seated for dinner immediately after arrival. The food I barely remember, my memory of the event dominated by the shot-glass-size helpings of aquavit (vodka) sitting by every place. I knew that the tiniest amount would do me in, but when I proceeded to sip gingerly, the hostess chided me loudly, "It is Swedish custom to quickly swallow the whole glassful." My polite protest that I was in the last stages of a bad head cold was overridden. "You've lived in Sweden, dear, so you surely know that what I'm requesting is simply good manners. So drink up. *Skål!*"

I obliged, whereupon my head began throbbing fiercely. I could only hope that this would be the last round of drinks, or that the hostess would make an exception for me. But, no. Refills all around, and the expectations were clearly the same. While everyone else tossed back their aquavit promptly, I hesitated, still hoping our hostess would defer to poor, under-the-weather me. But she was wholly insensitive to my plight, saying to my husband, "Surely you and your wife learned proper etiquette at parties in Sweden." He assured her we had, while I protested politely but in vain that I recalled no such requirement.

As I tipped the glass to my mouth, I surveyed the other guests at the table; all of them were following the protocol. And no help was forthcoming from my husband, whose eye I tried repeatedly but in vain to catch. My head, by now, felt like it was going to explode. I needed to be coddled, not lectured. Somehow, though, I finished the second glassful of aquavit.

Food was then served, and with it, wine. As my glass was being filled, feeling desperate as well as ill by this time, I had a crazy inspiration. I would ask to be excused; call home briefly on a house phone I had glimpsed in the kitchen (cell phones being very rare at that time); ask our sitter to call me and report a domestic emergency. I got myself excused, realizing as I rose from my chair how dizzy my swollen sinuses were making me. Sense of urgency renewed, I hastened to the kitchen, only to encounter a woman (a maid or cook, perhaps) sitting there. More bad luck, as my scheme had no room in it for a witness.

So, foiled, head pounding, I returned slowly to the table. "Anything wrong?" the hostess asked, and without waiting for an answer, she continued her conversation with another guest. From which she proceeded seamlessly to other conversations, while I labored to eat my dinner, conversing desultorily with the guests on either side of me.

Eventually, we made our goodbyes. On our way home, my husband and I discussed our hostess' behavior. My husband, a stoic about colds, felt I should have followed the protocol, been a better sport. I, of course, disagreed, pointing out that we'd attended plenty of dinner parties in Sweden, which we weren't required to begin by chugalugging aquavit.

In fairness to a country and a people who've provided us with many good experiences, I should say that our hostess' unempathetic behavior on that ill-fated evening was not—in my experience—common Swedish practice. Was she testing me in some peculiar way? Did I look like a good target? I never saw her again, as we soon moved to another university town, so I'll never know.

I Want to Thrive
Linda Hopkins

As I write this, my nineteenth wedding anniversary is next month. I reflect on having spent almost two decades of my life living and partnering with my husband. After all this time, my husband feels like a stranger to me. So much has happened during our years together, and yet the years have passed and we have not taken the time to develop a healthy, resilient relationship. Instead, I am at the brink of letting go of believing we could create something beautiful together.

We have lived side-by-side in the same house, in the same city, for two decades. My husband has been a partner in a successful business and has been a provider for our family of four. During our decades together, I had many roles outside the home. I was a science teacher, volunteered in my children's classrooms, and was a founding member of a scout group. I currently host women's groups and have a writing practice.

My husband and I parented side-by-side. As parents, we read to our children before bed. Supporting our children's interests in sports, music, story, and school, we spent hours organizing, and planning, and driving the children to activities. Parenting together, we set boundaries and consequences that created a safe environment for our children to grow up and to develop healthy relationships and participate in vibrant communities. Our teenage children are responsible, kind, and engaged human beings who are finding their way in this rapidly changing world.

And yet, with all the effort we have put into our children and into our careers and volunteer work, we have not cultivated a relationship that is supportive and loving. We have not modeled love at the center of our family unit. The question I ask myself is, "Can I find compassion for myself, and for my husband, and true understanding about how we could have arrived here, after nearly twenty years?"

Could it be that we both felt confined by our role as wife and mother/husband and father, in the context of our family? Was it my trauma, and his ADD that interfered in connecting with each other? Is it possible that the models our parents provided as husband and wife were so challenging to work from that our struggle to learn new ways was just too difficult? Has our society created so many unhealthy messages about how we are to be in relationship with ourselves and others, that we find it almost impossible to develop healthy practices? Could it be the entrenched patriarchal systems that overlay all of our thoughts, actions, and values, which make it nearly impossible to embrace our personal power, to be in right relationship to one another, and actively live a life of love?

I believe that all of those are true.

While my husband and I were living separate lives together, I have been teaching myself how to be in right relationship with others, and with myself. I have learned to find joy within myself. I have learned to love. These teachings have come from the Earth, not from the humans in my life. I have learned these lessons in the garden, watching the plants, observing the animals, watching the rain and the sun and the stars. I have learned joy and love by taking my place in right relationship with the living earth that sustains my life.

I do not do this alone. There are humans who assist, and guide, and walk with me on my journey towards healing and wholeness. These people claim their power as individuals, and then without giving or taking power from me, we sit side-by-side and take our place with each other. We witness and listen. We share and speak our truth. These human beings are learning to be in right relationship with the more than human world and with each other. We are healing individually and together as a community, healing ourselves and healing our planet.

These safe places for healing are hidden in our society. The dominant belief is that having power over ourselves, having power over others, and having power over the living planet is the way to survive in this world. This patriarchal way of thinking has been taught to me since birth. And it is my survival strategy.

I have been schooled to allow men to have power over me. I have been schooled to have power over others and over the earth. I recognize that in addition to being taught the patriarchy by men, I was taught this survival strategy by women as well.

The patriarchy is alive and well in me. I participate in the patriarchy every day. It is not something I am proud of, and it is something I am learning to speak the truth about. It is not until I can speak my truth about it, that I will be free.

When I first learned about the patriarchy, I reacted with anger towards the men in my life and in my family. How could they treat me this way? And yet, as I spent more and more time unpacking the reactions in my body to how I treat men, to how I allow them to treat me, to how I expect them to treat me, I realize that we are all indoctrinated into the patriarchy. We are all in this together. And if, as women, we don't speak our truth about how we too are living out the patriarchy, we will never be able to shift this way of being in our bodies, in our families, in our communities, and on our planet.

I have personal power. I have strength. I carry the wisdom passed to me through my ancestors. And yet, I hide my power. I hide my strength. I deny the wisdom in my body. Why? Because the culture, in subtle and not subtle ways, sends the message that women are powerless, women are weak, women are not wise. I have been immersed in this messaging since I was in my mother's womb.

In my private life, with myself and with other women, I can see the truth. But in my marriage, in my family, in my community, I fear coming out as the powerful, strong and wise woman that I am. I fear it because of the consequences experienced by other women who have come before me when they stepped into their power, when they showed their strength, when they shared their wisdom. Deep in my body, I fear what might happen if I show up as my true self.

Most of us take part in the patriarchal system without even knowing it. Whether we are women or men in our society, many of us struggle to find belonging in our families and in our communities when we show up as our true self. Women and men alike have been socialized to play out roles that support the patriarchal way of being on this planet. We keep the secret of our true selves to ourselves, because if we did present our true selves, we would not fit in with the norms of our social programming.

Not only do we keep our own true selves from showing up, we also influence others to hide. We are silencing each other in order to keep ourselves safe in this culture. And that stifles understanding.

I am done surviving—I want to thrive. What this looks like, I do not know. But I am listening, I am watching, and I am learning from the Living Earth. Life and the systems that support life on earth contain the answers to living in right relationship with ourselves, with our partners, in our families and in our communities. I am ready to learn a new way, are you?

My Mother and Her Pain
Len Leatherwood

"Please don't share our family tragedy," my mother whispered to me while we stood in church together in Pottsboro, Texas, in 1990.

I understood what she was saying to me. "Please don't tell these people. I can't bear to deal with this right now."

Tragedy was not too strong of a word. We had just learned that my oldest brother had been diagnosed with AIDS. He had told us himself the words that encapsulated the situation: "The nurse came in and said, 'We have two different types of medication. One that works for some, one that works for others. If those don't work for you, then you need to know now that we don't use respirators.'"

Death was what AIDS spelled at that time. Protease inhibitors would come too late for brother John and his fight for life. He died in 1991, a little over a year after his official diagnosis.

My mother called him every day when he was sick but visited him only rarely in Dallas, 60 miles from her home. When our brother Jim suggested John move to LA for better treatment, my mother encouraged him to go but did not come out to see him once he was here. Instead, she continued her routine of daily calls and saw other young men with AIDS for free in her counseling practice, listening with her trained ear to their pain and their isolation.

My brother seemed to understand. "Nothing would be more like hell to me than to see Mother standing over my bed, ready to change my adult diaper." They had a clear-cut relationship: adoration at a distance.

My mother was a woman who walked out of a movie if it upset her. She stood right up and stomped out. "I just couldn't bear it," were words I heard from her on many occasions. Reality seemed to sap her of energy; cruelty was something that threatened to send her over the edge.

Her common method of escape from the persistent ugliness of life was Scotch. A glass or two or three or four in the evening helped soften all the ragged edges, or so it must have seemed to her. As for me, her retreat appeared to create more problems than solutions. She became critical when she drank, often shifting her gaze in my direction: the daughter who so reminded her of her husband, who she described as someone who "swept her off her feet," but who had fallen short in the long run with his impeccable people versus book skills. She was a woman who believed in books, needed books to bring her out of her malaise.

Her method of dealing with my father was not unlike the method she used in church that day so long ago. Silence was her watchword. When in doubt, she stood up and walked out. No words at all. She simply retreated.

Ironically, my mother was a great communicator. She was a gifted therapist and a fine writer. She knew exactly how to verbalize someone else's pain, as long as the pain didn't get too close to her. If that happened, then she headed upstairs to her office to read or to write. No need to sully the experience with too much talk.

Now, as a mother myself, I understand not wanting to casually chat about a tragic diagnosis. How heartbreaking. How devastating. No need to stand at coffee hour enlisting support from other parishioners. The pain was too raw, too deep. Now, I understand my mother so much better than I did then. I see so clearly her pain, her disappointment, her utter defeat. She had no words to convey the tragedies in her life; she had no need to see "movie" tragedies when hers felt so acute.

And yet, she kept right on living. Past her husband's death, and then one son, followed by another. Her own life ended before two more of her children would die long before their time.

Perhaps on some deep level, she already knew. Perhaps she was grieving in advance.

Perhaps "Don't share our family tragedy," stood for all the tragedies to come.

But as for me, I must err on the other side. I share and share and share. This is my way of making sense of cruelty and inequity. This is my way of coping with loss. But, then again, I have never lost a child. I may be struck stone silent if I ever do.

I only hope I can remember that making Scotch my comfort food will not help.

My mother finally stopped drinking. She took up gambling instead. But only for fun and that was a good thing. She and her friend laughed when they played Black Jack; their chuckles still bring a smile to my face.

I loved my mother. I still love her deeply.

Who knows the pain that lurks under the surface?

We all best be kind-hearted.

SWEETHEART
Catherine N. Steinberg

She was one of the beautiful people…tall, slim, long dark hair coiled up perfectly at the back of her head. Her black summer dress hugged her body nicely and was accompanied by a three-tier coral bracelet on her right arm and a diamond-studded wedding ring on her left hand. Black flats hung loosely from her feet as she folded one knee over the other. She toyed with eating the fruit salad that had been sitting in a fancy takeaway carton as she perused the *New York Times*.

A workman slid in on the seat beside her. She looked stunned for a moment at the intrusion. *Didn't this fellow know she owned the whole*

G.D. seat? She tried to busy herself with paper and pen, but kept being distracted with the movements of her fellow passenger. Then her cell phone rang, relieving her from this unwelcome situation. "Sweetheart..." she said, and then lost the signal. After several more attempts, she finally reconnected with the caller and offered sympathetic remarks to "Sweetheart's" apparently terrible day. Other brief superficial business was conducted regarding her successful shopping trip in the city, ending with a mild disagreement about which flight to take to Cabo. She concluded her part of the discussion warning she was "tired tonight."

I wanted to shout, *Well, aren't we all tired?! Especially those of us who work for a living and barely can afford this train ride, which by the way is my vacation out of somewhere!* I thought to say this and more. What hardship has she suffered besides sharing a seat with a stranger clearly not from her walk of life? What loss or disappointment has she endured? I refrained from saying these things. And a good thing, too, since when our eyes caught for a brief moment, I could see her hollowed loneliness and the lines of worry around her flat lips. A life hard-lived despite the comforts of privilege. Maybe she, too, wanted to shout.

WHY DID YOU SAY THAT?
Marian McCaa Thomas

THE SCENE:

A public swimming pool in Kansas City, Missouri, the summer of 1974.

THE PEOPLE:

Me and my two little white boys, and my friend and her two little black girls.

THE CONVERSATION:

ME: "Do you think there will ever come a time when the races will intermingle so that everyone will be a neutral beige color?" (I had been observing how very pale my white boys looked in the swimming pool, compared to my friend's black children. For some reason, the contrast made me feel uncomfortable.)

MY FRIEND: "My children are fine just the way they are!"

The tone of her voice made me realize that I had offended her, but it was too late to take back my words. We were members of a church which was racially integrated, with people of different economic backgrounds, and our pastor, her husband, was a black man from Bermuda, where growing up he had not experienced animosity or prejudice from the white people living there. The pool where we were swimming had been integrated years earlier, but as a result very few white people used the pool anymore. In fact, that day, my boys and I were the only whites using the pool, which was quite crowded.

Having been involved in civil rights actions in the south, having decided along with my husband to keep our children in the public schools from which whites were fleeing, and having been part of a racially integrated congregation for years, I had thought of myself as being enlightened on matters of racial prejudice. Back then, the term "white supremacy" was not used the way it is today. It has taken me almost fifty years to fully understand why my friend reacted the way she did!

My friend grew up in the Boston area, where prejudice against Blacks was alive and well. She had been taught well by her parents that she was worthy, beautiful, and deeply loved. She had a built-in shield against the treatment she would receive her entire life. To her, my words felt like yet another attempt to belittle her children, even though that had not been my intent. But why, I asked myself recently, had I felt it was okay to say what I did?

I realize now that my words were spoken from a position of feeling confident of my place in society as a white person. It would not matter if my children became a little less white—beige, say—because they would still be "safe" in beige skins. But it mattered to my friend to celebrate her children's Blackness as beautiful, as God-given "rightness," because she had to affirm that her family deserved to be appreciated the way they were. She was refusing to feel humiliated!

It is truly difficult to see through another's eyes. My friend never brought up that conversation through the years, but I recently reminded her of it and apologized for my lack of understanding her situation. She was loving enough to accept my apology and to remain a good friend. She showed more empathy for me than I had shown her so many years ago.

TALKING ABOUT BUFFALO WITH THE DEAD
Christina M. Wells

Sometimes when I close my eyes, I see myself at eight, as if I am a separate person from who I am now. I wear purple pants and a purple striped shirt, and I have left third grade early. It's Wednesday, and my dad teaches out of town on Wednesdays. My mom is also at work, so I am at my grandparents' house. I sit across the bar from my grandmother on a swivel stool, turning on it, while a basket of popcorn sits between us. Copper pots and pans hang from a rack on the ceiling overhead, and a kitchen witch dangles over the sink. I don't remember what we talk about in this memory. The picture may be a composite sketch of everything we ever said—it may be the day I call up that stands for everything. Where do I stand when I watch myself from the outside? Perhaps I am in front of my grandparents' fireplace, warm, solid, and middle-aged.

My grandmother, a woman of largely Western and Central European descent, did a lot of work for racial equality and the poor. In places where I have written about this before, it almost seems as though I am listing her personal tropes, the stories we tell when we talk about Grandma. I would get compared to her sometimes when I was growing up, especially if I got riled up by bigots at school or found something to be unfair. Some years after the scene above, I wrote about the Civil War for a camp play, and someone called me my "grandmother's granddaughter." I spent a lot of time talking to her, so it's not surprising there would be a connection in our values.

This morning, I thought of this scene, like I have thought of it so often recently. My wife Jen and I drove past a large church on the Little River Turnpike, morning caffeine hot in our hands. The church's electronic sign was blinking solidarity with the people of Texas, who have lost so many children and their teachers. I cried for those faces in the paper. I thought of the children who wouldn't live a natural span of years, and I cried for the teachers who wouldn't, either. I could feel something of the siblings and parents who went looking for children and didn't find them.

I also looked at the sign with frustration and anger. Someone took time to set up this blinking sign, and it took time to assemble letters on other, more low-tech signs. People work hard to display grief publicly, pulling together the parts of themselves that understand what it is to lose something as a civilization. Would it diminish the losses of Texas if someone acknowledged the other losses of the past ten days? We are passing through a very long time of civilian loss with military grade guns, and most of us hope that it ends with something more like peace.

When we passed the sign, I had tears passing beneath my sunglasses, thinking of what my grandmother would say, about both the children and the adults lost this week. Black people died in Buffalo, New York, shot down the same week as all those precious children. They were buying groceries, the kind of venture that is less a destination and more a stop on the way to somewhere else. A hate crime met them in the in-between—that place between one part of the day and another.

For some reason, when I heard about these losses, I thought about an older woman pushing a cart from aisle to aisle, thinking about something to prepare for family and friends. I imagined her with plans to be somewhere else. Isn't everyone planning to be somewhere else?

I think of this imaginary woman, even when I see pictures of the actual victims, and find no one exactly like her. For me, she is a kind of Everywoman, out in her neighborhood. She never falls, but I cry when I see her in my mind, just the same. She is someone out there, shopping on a Saturday. Maybe no one knows who she is. Maybe they won't.

I imagine picking up the phone and calling my grandmother. I can hear the phone ring, and I can see her split-second decision to walk down the hall instead of answering the phone in the kitchen. I see her hustle to the hall phone, where she clears her throat before answering. Then, we talk about the list of victims, and maybe we talk about how few people seem to be talking about them. Maybe we even talk about some of them, wondering at the lives they lived outside the tiny margins of a magazine.

I see this like it could happen, though my grandmother is dead. She lived a natural life and died at an old age, and I still find I want to talk to her about all of this death and all of this dying. In fact, she taught a course about death and dying. I am unsure whether it would have covered American grieving practices, those we openly cry for, and those we don't, at least not collectively.

I sit in the guest room/office at my house, the one we call the Grandma room. It's her favorite color of purple. She made one of the wall hangings, and she gave me another, a framed poster of a woman protesting. I think about this. Grieving for children is its own ball of wax, but of course, we grieve for all ages of people. I grieve for my grandmother, who may have been older when she died than any of the victims at the grocery store.

My grandmother made me a protester, even though I'm kind of quiet about it. I think about putting this into a page with the right margins, pasting it into a box where I can submit it somewhere. That's different, to be sure, from screaming with a sign somewhere. The people I want to reach are quiet, though. They are people living their days, doing their things. They may be so overwhelmed by the past few weeks—years, really—that they could miss a news item without any malintent. We miss people. We pass them all the time without really seeing them. I suppose we could miss a mass shooting, since we've had so many of them that our bodies are begging us not to see.

I miss my grandmother, and for all I know of spirituality, I may pass her, too, without seeing her. What I can definitively say is that when we sat at the kitchen bar with our popcorn and talked about the world, I hoped there were more people like her than there actually are. I don't mean to suggest she was perfect. But what I do mean is that she talked to people of all races and ethnicities. She wanted everyone to have an education and to be safe. These seem like no-brainer things, and they even seemed like no-brainer things to me back then, happy to be out of school early so I could have a real conversation with my grandmother instead of a kinda fake one with an elementary school teacher in Arkansas.

But I wonder how many people understand the basics of equity, as I pass signs that recognize one mass shooting when they could recognize two, or three, or twelve. In the same town where my grandmother worked with Black people, I went to school dances where Black and White kids sometimes shuffled their feet on opposite sides of the room with no one saying much about it. Much can coexist in the same place—movements forward, movements back. Dances in place.

There is time enough to grieve for everyone. It is a constant buzzing sensation I feel when I write, when I walk, when I sleep. I miss my grandmother. I also miss the chance to talk about ten Black people who we didn't know, whose names will likely be forgotten, if they haven't been already. I miss knowing more people who want to talk about people in a different community from theirs. I miss being a little girl in braids, who thought it a bigger, more expansive world out there, than it actually seems to be.

WISHES
Ariela L. Zucker

"I wish things were easier," I said to my friend Naomi one day. We sat next to a small round table in the university coffee shop, sipping coffee and digging into huge slices of apple pie.

"Who does not?" she replied, shrugging her shoulders, concentrating on an especially big piece on her plate.

I like Naomi's matter-of-fact attitude. She never seems unnerved by the challenges that life throws at her. She is always calm and collected. She, unlike me, employs reason as her first line of defense, rather than emotions.

"Don't you ever get upset or frustrated?" I tried again. "Look around you; there is so much injustice and chaos, so many bad and sad things, and a sea of stupidity."

Naomi just smiled at me with a mouth full of pie and waved her hand towards the big glass windows.

"What?" I turned in that direction, but all I saw were the trees outside and, far away in the distance, the skyline of Jerusalem. "What are you looking at?" I turned back to her. "I don't see anything."

For a long time, the small cafeteria on the first floor of the library building on Jerusalem's Mt. Scopus campus has been one of my favorite spots. Every time I visit Jerusalem, I try to find some reason to visit the bookstore on the second floor and treat myself to a leisurely coffee, preferably with a good friend. Naomi has been my friend since we were in fifth grade. Looking at her sitting across from me reminded me of so many things: school, girl scouts, my years in the army, old friends, and long-lost friendships. It was almost a miracle that we remained friends after so many years.

I looked at her and tried again. "Remember the days we used to walk home together after school and talk about life?" She nodded her head, and her eyes looked straight through me. "Life, the future, and making decisions," she chuckled. "We were so young and sure we could make a difference; little did we know," she smiled at me, recalling that time in her mind.

"Remember what we used to wish for?" I kept probing.

"That we can have a cup of coffee on Mt. Scopus looking through the windows at the outline of Jerusalem?" She said it jokingly, but her eyes were serious.

I looked at the window again. The sun was low on the horizon, and its rays touched the golden dome of the rock, turning it into pure gold. Behind it, I could make out parts of the wall surrounding the city and, further away, already getting hazy in the dusk, the tall modern buildings of the new city.

"Remember how we used to stand on the old Notre Dame Monastery balcony looking at the walls surrounding the old town, wondering if we would ever get to see the inside and the Wailing Wall?"

"I remember the first time I made it to Mt. Scopus and saw the town from the other side. That was different," Naomi laughed, but there was a hint of sadness in her voice.

"So, just like in the stories, we got what we wished for, but…" I was unsure where I was going with this thought.

"We were always told that seeing things from a different angle is good for a more balanced perspective," Naomi continued as if she did not hear me and talked to herself. "In this case, it did not work; it did not lead to a greater understanding."

The setting sun took the colors with it. My cup was cold when I touched it. The remaining pie on my plate was colorless and tasteless. The day had lost its color, as if a large cloud covered the sun and made everything look bleak.

"Let's go," I said to Naomi, who was still gazing at the windows and seemed deep in thought.

"Do you ever think," she said, as if continuing my sentence, "how things could have turned out if this wish had not been granted?"

I thought of the many years of living in a divided town. A town with a wall running through its midst, separating us from all our sacred places. I thought about the other years, when the wall was no longer there. Walls create a physical divide, but people do the rest.

CALLING OUT FOR CARING

PROGENY
Lin Brummels

> I'm suddenly tired, never been this tired of this
> question that's always asked if you're a woman.
> Do you have children?
> — *Susan Browne*

Both grandmothers
died when I was too young
to remember them,
and I have no sense of their place.
I always get questions
when I meet someone
my age or older,
and often now
from anyone over fifty,
Do you have grandchildren? or
How many grandchildren do you have?
And from those who just assume
everyone has them,
How old are your grandkids?
When I answer in the negative
and joke about grand-dogs,
the next comment
is always, *I'm so sorry,*
as if I should be pitied
for having children
who have not reproduced. I can
only imagine the pressure
my daughter and daughter-in-law
feel with society's incessant pushing.
As if raising offspring is a woman's
only useful contribution.

East Young Avenue
Joan L. Connor

The realtor was my husband's grandson and the rumor spread quickly. I might consider a generous offer on my 900-square-foot home, in downtown Coeur d'Alene, Idaho. It had curb appeal with flower boxes, turquoise Adirondack chairs on the doll-sized deck, a Little Free Library box painted green and white to match. The proposal was accompanied by an emotional appeal. "Our family will create memories in your home," their attached letter pleaded.

> weeds knee high
> gapping fence
> "House for Rent"
> my quick drive by
> reveals The Truth

DYSCALCULIA
B. Lynn Goodwin

Fisher Tisher knew the ropes. It was his third time in Algebra I. He sat in back, watching the numbers bump like pool balls. What was the key?

"Ms. Bowen? Ms. Bowen?"

"Yes, Fisher."

"Nothing. I just like saying your name."

Laughter.

Applause.

Bows to the audience.

Referral slip.

Detention.

And who was running detention that day?

"Ms. Bowen? Ms. Bowen?"

"Yes, Fisher?"

"Nothing. I just like…."

"I like doing Algebra. Since we're the only ones here, let's do a few problems together, okay?"

His eyes were moist as he shrugged.

LINES
Teresa Lynn

The lines are long and the workers are slow
In this place on the other side of town,
The only one with an appointment today,
Disrupting my nice convenient life
With dirty women and crying babies—
I'm careful to keep my distance.

Outside a car backfires and women fall
Like overripe plums from a tree,
Soft flesh plopping, bruising,
Somehow tucking the children,
Every one now silent as death,
Beneath themselves with outrageous grace.

They look about warily, pick themselves up slowly,
Brush off their children matter-of-factly,
A hard thread binding them in common,
While I alone, left standing
Am slow to comprehend the reason and
Cannot fathom the fear nor the resilience.

The lines are long and the workers are tired
In this place on the other side of town,
Where women are strong as trees and children
Have learned when to shut up or else.
Both sorrow and awe fill my soul
As I reach for the hand of my neighbor.

I See You
Lucy Painter

We no longer see each other in person, my cousin Bobby and me. The telephone is our connection now, words passed back and forth to honor the link we have had since we were both children in Virginia many years ago. Other cousins have drifted away, but not us. Now we talk about something we both know all too well—a cruel disease called Parkinson's.

Bobby's wife, Ducky, was diagnosed in 2019 and has reached, in what seems record time, stage 5. Paralysis, dementia, sleeplessness, only some of the horrors she suffers. Once a vibrant, brilliant woman who worked at the Library of Congress and knew something about almost every book in that huge collection, she now needs help with getting through each day. She often doesn't know her own children, or her husband, who is her caretaker.

This life Bobby lives is what we talk about now, how he manages the bathing, the feeding, the sleepless nights. We talk about how he misses her, the woman who bore their two children, who crewed with him on their boat sailing the Chesapeake, the rivers of Virginia, the Gulf. The boat is gone, no time to sail now, he tells me. Each day he lives with loss.

I understand. My brother Madison was diagnosed with the same devastating disease in 2003. Unlike Ducky, he did well for almost 15 years, only gradually losing his balance, his sense of taste and smell, his ability to drive. His progression was slow, offering us futile hope that researchers would find a cure, that he had been misdiagnosed, that one day he would wake up and walk with the same steady, strong gait I knew.

Madison had been my friend, my champion, for as long as I could remember. He never pushed me away as his twin often did. He listened to me, to my teenage drama over this boyfriend or that, warning me away from some he knew were trouble. He encouraged me to go to college, as he did, to get out of the dead town we both grew up in, as he did. All through our adult years, we talked each Sunday evening on the phone for hours, sharing memories, commiserating about worries over our children, our spouses, and our parents as they aged.

It was during the phone calls, I realized the Madison I knew and loved was leaving. His voice wavered, his memory failed, and sometimes he was irritable, impatient with me. Sometimes he hung up on me without warning.

I visited him, driving to Richmond where he lived. His body shrunken, his hands trembling violently, I watched him try to walk through the kitchen and stumble with each step, his three-footed cane useless. The next time I saw him, he was in a wheelchair, blind, skeletal. He did not know me.

I sat with him, along with his wife and son, in the hospice on Grace Street in Richmond, one block off Monument Avenue. His breath came in gasps, his fingers twitched when I touched them, and I have always wondered—did he know me, know that we were there?

He died the next morning, 3:30 a.m., when we had all gone home. I don't tell Bobby this story, about those final excruciating hours by Madison's bedside. It is what he now faces. I will be there when he does.

My Mother, the Poet
Janet Grace Riehl

Mom, since you misplaced parts of your mind, you have become a poet. Did you know that, Mama? Bet you didn't! Metaphors are your métier now.

When I called this morning, you answered, voice hoarse and croaking with flu. "I have a frog in my throat," you told me, laughing. "Perhaps even two or three!"

"Well, I certainly hope they jump out soon," I said. And you laughed again.

I like you as a poet, Mom. We have more fun together. Life isn't so serious for you now. Ruth Evelyn Johnston Thompson, family strategist and survivor—I hardly know you in your mind's new flights of fancy.

And, strangely, you hardly know yourself. You are searching for the Ruth you knew once. This new Ruth has left old rhymes and rhythms behind. One thing is certain though. Your new life as a poet opens a whole new world, a world of ever-new discovery for all of us. Your poetic, floating world travels in the time and space of your mind, and it has come up with metaphor to explain all the mystery.

Waking up the day after a brain bleed not knowing where you were, what had happened, or who you were, could have made a girl feel funny. But your internal translator took right over. You knew that when a gal feels like a stranger in a strange land, there is one surefire way to cope with what's going on: plan a trip! Or better yet, take a trip! You, who traveled the world throughout your lifetime, now return in your mind to far-off places—without passport or itinerary.

After every trip you took together, you and Pop wrote exhaustive reports with details only a private detective could remember. The trip reports expanded into informal travel guides. You told family and friends how you got there, where you stayed, how much your food and lodging cost, and the history of the place. You listed the name of every bird you saw (your part of the report, Mom) and every person you talked to (Pop's part of the report).

In your poetic phase now, you continue on in the tradition of the trip report. Gazing out the window at the snow-covered trees, you say, "Ah, I'm enjoying this beautiful weather in Brazil. Aren't you? Don't you love how all the women wear sleeveless blouses that show their bosoms?" My sister has cautioned me not to take my conversations with you as literal exchanges of fact. But I know a poet when I hear one, so we're on the same wavelength.

Despite the dementia journeying through your brain, you are crystal clear on the essential facts. When the doctor asked you where you were, you said, quite plainly: "Here!" On a follow-up question, when they asked, "Where is your home?" you knew what a foolish question it was and answered succinctly, "Not here!"

Over the holidays, when I visited you in the skilled nursing facility, you rhapsodized as you remembered your breakfast, a look of soft satisfaction around your mouth. "Lots of food. Pancakes, eggs, oatmeal. Free, too; it's all free! Have you found a good place for us to have breakfast tomorrow morning?"

"Well, Mother, this sounds like a good place to stay. Let's eat breakfast here in the morning." And then I asked, "Do you know where you are, Mom? You're at Rosewood in Alton, Illinois."

"Where?"

"Rosewood."

I broke the word down for you as if we were in Mexico or Holland again, learning a foreign language.

"What smells good?" I cupped my hand to support a phantom stem and brought the blossom up to my nose for an appreciative sniff.

"A rose," you said, you who had been a gardener extraordinaire. You, still the brilliant student. Wheeling you in your chair along the hallway, I tapped the rose-colored walls. "Rose," I repeated.

Sighting a wooden bathroom door on our stroll, I took a chance that no one was sitting inside on the toilet and gave it a rap.

"Wood," I said. "Rosewood. A skilled nursing facility in Alton, Illinois. Something like a hospital."

"Oh. Where are we staying tonight?"

"You are staying here, Mom. I'm going back to the house to stay overnight with Pop."

"Where are you sleeping?"

"Up in the pink room, Mom."

"Janet, go to the closet and get my red dress. Put my walker in the car. I'm going home with you."

"Mom, I can't do that. You need to stay here until you get stronger and it's safe for you to come home."

You leaned toward me and whispered, just we two conspirators together. "Janet, help me break out of this hoosegow. Janet, where's the door?!"

Mom, poet-trail boss, still masterminding, even through the broken synapses. Mom, poet-cowgirl, planning her jailbreak. Mom, ready to flee this hoosegow on horseback with me, her youngest daughter, as trusty sidekick. Off on another adventure!

I grinned and saddled up for the ride.

THE THIN CURTAIN
Elena Schwolsky

The first day I spent on the Oncology floor, I was alone in a two-bedded room. Through the window, if I craned my neck just so, I could catch a glimpse of sky. I had shape-shifted several times since I felt a tender lump in my abdomen several months earlier—from retired nurse, to anxious patient waiting for the results of biopsies, to a woman with a diagnosis of Stage 3 Ovarian cancer.

Major surgery had left my body looking like a construction site. A zippered scar bisected my belly and there was a hollow feeling where multiple organs and tumors had been. A month later, after my first dose of chemotherapy, I was back in the hospital with a serious infection—my left eye swollen shut, red and angry.

Because of COVID, visitors were limited to two per day, masked and distant. My husband came in the late afternoon, but by nightfall I was alone again. In the middle of the night, I was awakened by the sound of a stretcher being wheeled into my room and the quiet murmur of voices. The thin beige curtain that separated the beds rustled with activity, and then quiet and darkness returned to the room.

In the morning, a woman in colorful African dress waved to me on my way to the bathroom.

"I'm Jamila," she said. "This is my daughter, Layla."

Layla's eyes were large and round in her dark face. She was swallowed up by the bed like a tiny colorful bird, her headwrap bright against the white of her pillow. "I'm Elena," I said, hoping they could sense the smile under my mask.

The next afternoon, Layla was sitting up on a video call with her family, laughing with her young daughter. "She's fourteen months," she responded to my question. "I'll show you her picture tomorrow." But that night, after hours of moaning from behind the curtain, Layla was wheeled out on a stretcher. I thought I would never see her again, but two days later she was back. She smiled as I passed, and remembered my name. "I'm better," she said. She didn't look better, but then neither did I, when I caught sight of my disfigured face and rapidly disappearing hair in the mirror above the sink.

By that time the nurses on the floor knew that I was a retired nurse and they were taking good care of me. My eye was improving, but Layla was getting sicker. In the middle of the night, she used the call bell on the remote like a walkie-talkie, calling out *Hello Hello Nurse Nurse Someone please help me* in a schoolgirlish soprano. She was nauseated. She needed to use the bedpan. She was in pain. Once or twice, she called my name…*Lena, Lena*. But all I could do was add the press of my own call button to her urgent pleas.

The floor was impossibly busy and short-staffed. When the nurses finally came, they looked exhausted. Layla was combative. *You don't come when I call. Why don't you come?* They drew away from her, defensive. *You're not our only patient you know.* My fingers curled into a fist on the bed. Why were they talking to her that way? Couldn't they tell how young she was, how scared? Were they distancing themselves from Layla and her family, with their African garb and essential oils, staying away from her pain and anger?

I had thought I understood Layla. After all, we were on the same journey—struggling with the discomfort and uncertainty of cancer. But now I wondered. A bond of suffering united us, but was that enough? Perhaps I was ignoring all the things that separated us—where we had come from, the lives we would return to. Perhaps I didn't really understand at all.

The next day, the curtain clung to Jamila's round body as she tended to her daughter. Layla smiled big as I wobbled past. She seemed happy and held up a picture of her daughter, but I couldn't see it clearly with my one open eye.

I heard the soft voice of a doctor on the other side of the curtain as I settled back in bed. His tone was gentle. He sounded kind.

"Are you in any pain?" he asked.

Not now.

"What do you understand about your cancer?"

Layla spoke in a low voice. I felt like an eavesdropper but there was nowhere for me to go.

"Your cancer's getting worse," the doctor said. "None of the treatments are working. We've run out of options. Do you understand?"

He paused. *Wait*, I whispered in my head—*please wait*. His casual tone belied the gravity of the information he was relaying. Did Layla realize that he was telling her she was dying, that she would, perhaps soon, leave her daughter without a mother? This news was being delivered to her during rounds in the middle of a busy floor, with only a thin curtain providing a shred of privacy. *Wait*, I thought. *Let her search for her questions. Give her time to find her feelings.*

But the doctor moved on quickly, heading out of the room. At the door he paused.

"Are you in any pain right now?"

No.

"I'll be back tomorrow."

Fine.

I lay in my bed for the rest of that day, an involuntary witness to what should have been a private and intimate exchange. I wanted to part the curtain, to reach across to Layla, to let her know I was there, that I cared. Part of my role as a nurse had been delivering this kind of news to families. I had cried with them, sat with them beside the beds of their dying children, attended their funerals. But now I was a patient, held in place by IV poles and infection. What could I do?

My husband came in the early evening. He straightened the bedside table, rubbed my feet, and put his cool hand on my forehead as he said goodnight. Jamila sat silent—eyes closed, her daughter's small hand resting in hers. She left soon after my husband did, and Layla and I were alone—toiling to get through yet another night.

When I woke the next morning, Layla was gone. "She's been moved to a different room," the nurses said. I thought about her all through the day, and the next night, as I lay alone in the darkness. I was just starting this cancer journey—a white, middle-class professional with the tools and resources to navigate our fragmented health system. I had hope for renewed strength and health, perhaps even a cure. Layla was perhaps nearing the end of her life—a young mother, drowning in pain and fear, an African immigrant to a new land that was not always welcoming.

It's been several months since my hospital stay. I have resumed chemotherapy and am dealing with the rollercoaster ride of symptoms and challenges my treatment presents one day at a time. Two variant surges have served as a forceful reminder that COVID is still with us and, like so many others, I've moved deeper into hibernation for the winter. I'm almost two-thirds of the way through my treatment, looking forward to life after chemo.

I think of Layla often, wondering how she is and if she's surviving still. Maybe the doctors have found a treatment that will work for her. Or maybe her family is mourning her loss. Our paths will probably never cross again, but for three nights and three days we had shared a room and glimpses into each other's lives. Together we had been lifted up by a little good news, by family visits, by feeling a bit stronger—and then plunged into endless worry and waiting. We had moved from our hospital beds into very different realities. But perhaps the thin curtain that marked a boundary between us still holds the memory of our lives in that brief moment when they intersected in the common labor of survival.

A Poem for Uvalde, Texas
Madeline Sharples

President Biden
Said losing a child
Is like tearing
A piece out of your soul.
I know. I lost a son.
Yesterday, nineteen
Sets of parents
In Uvalde, Texas,
Lost their precious
Little boys and girls, too.
No amount of prayers
Will ever take away
Their pain.
I know. My pain
Stays in my heart
After twenty-three years.
And that we allowed it
To happen.
That we didn't restrict
An eighteen-year-old
From buying
An assault weapon,
Designed and intended
Only to be used
In battlefields
And not to bloody
Schools or grocery stores
Or places of worship.
We must stop
These horrors –
The killing of
Innocent people
Just wanting
To live normal lives.
We must stop
The pain and
The pieces of our souls
From tearing away.

As Thyself
Monique S. Simón

Pearce watched the scenery of men and women going about their games of love with the same disinterest as he did the changing shades of green amidst the hillside peaks and valleys. It was all distant to him. As far away a view as his boyhood days, when his family had first moved to Oregon sometime in the early 1940s.

"Yes, perhaps we ought set here for a while," his mother had said that long ago day. Until those fateful words, the family was headed to a ranch somewhere in Northern California. But, the simple offer of some leftover cough medicine and beds of hay in the Musset's barn was enough to convince the travel-and-faith-weary family that perhaps the people here were cheerful types—the kind who held dear the commandment to 'love thy neighbor as thyself,' even when that neighbor was a tattered migrant family a few shades darker and a few meals weaker.

It wasn't long before the great rains followed by the cooler winds would signal Helen's final cough—the one that shook her tiny body until...

Here, grief was another opportunity to love thy neighbor. And like that, the Davidsons were just another family in a town of mourners and lovers, workers and worshippers.

Little Alfred was born not more than a year later. With his fragile health and sharp mind, he became a town celebrity. Somewhere, in other towns, ladies shopped for new dresses in pristine shops and ordered matching handbags from glossy catalogs while sampling scones. Here—amongst the cheerful, loving types—families delighted themselves in amassing tattered, dusty books, as fast as Alfred could devour them with his pristine mind.

Pearce was never jealous of Alfred. Never begrudged him the miracles of a much healthier adulthood—not his years on scholarship at Howard University, nor his success as a civil engineer for the big agricultural company in California.

Yet, as he read through the letter, detailing Alfred's new life with his soon-to-be wife, there was a twisting in his gut and tightening in his lungs. Pearce set aside the last page of the letter, hoping the slightest wind would carry it far from his imaginings. But as he half-heartedly secured the pages at the very edges with a light pebble of a rock, the softest breeze lifted the top pages and revealed a photograph.

Pearce was suddenly aware of the new feelings in his gut and lungs again. Just then, the breeze quickened, revealing a few sections of the last page. His eyes were too set in the direction of the woman's photograph to miss the lines of Alfred's ever-perfect penmanship: "make your acquaintance;" "young widow;" "cousin;" "loves the farm;" "two girls;" "if you agree."

Pearce didn't know his gut and lungs were capable of so many new feelings. Or that he could hear the sound of his own heart beating—full and fast and somehow light, like the slightest breeze could knock him still.

Can I Swim in Your Lane?
Catherine N. Steinberg

"Can I swim in your lane?" my 30-year-old son asked, as I gazed past him at the empty lanes of the community pool and thought, *why share my lane when he can have his own?* He was a better swimmer than I and won awards in this sport during his youth. These days we lived 3,000 miles apart, even after the death of his dad (my husband) last year. While there was much we shared during this lengthy visit, why my son preferred swimming alongside his mother was puzzling. But then, after looking into his face, I was able to see the small boy in the man I raised, and answered, "Of course!"

LETTER TO OUR INSOLENT SERVER
Rhonda Wiley-Jones

That February evening decades ago promised cool breezes as we schlepped through sand to a table in our favorite island restaurant. It provided daily-caught fish, wind from the ocean just feet away, music from lapping waves. My husband Lynn and I lounged in our Mexican paradise.

The busboy delivered chips and salsa to us, as was the custom. We were thirsty after a day in the sun. Impatiently, I bounced my leg and tapped my fingers for you, our server.

You flip-flopped through the sand to wait on others who arrived after we did.

The customer across the sandy aisle from us watched you snub us. "You don't get service here like we do in the States." I didn't say so, but I agreed.

Our menus lay closed in front of us to let you know we were ready. I had learned the custom of closing the menu while waiting tables in my twenties at a Shoney's Big Boy in Little Rock. It signaled the server one was ready to order. You disregarded us.

While working as a waiter, I earned low wages; tips were the lion's share of compensation. Since then I have tipped generously. One evening in graduate school, after dinner and embarrassed I did not have enough money, I left my server postage stamps, hoping she would appreciate the monetary value.

Back at our table that night in Mexico, Lynn hailed you with a raised hand. Next, I called out, "Señora!" on your return. You sauntered right past us in your swaying skirt, as if we were invisible. Others continued to arrive and you took their orders.

You were the only server, so understandably busy, yet we wondered aloud. "Maybe she sees our water bottles and assumes we'll not order drinks, reducing her tip. She's punishing us." "Perhaps she's new and doesn't know how to juggle tables as they're filled." "She could be having a bad day or a headache." We tried to make sense of you ignoring us.

You trekked by us as if time did not matter, almost in a daze. We huffed and puffed in our impatient arrogance, hoping that might attract your attention. It didn't. Trying to be generous in spirit, I decided to recalibrate expectations. "I came to Mexico to slow down."

Finally, after half-an-hour, you ambled to our table with a pencil tucked in your graying bun. Without acknowledging the delay or apologizing, your vacant eyes moved from the kitchen to other tables, as if we were an inconvenience. At Shoney's, one requirement of customer service was direct eye contact with a smile, so your indifference irritated me.

You served Lynn his beer, while I waited for my mixed drink, a margarita. Another Shoney's rule: drinks should come to the table at the same time.

Finally, you brought dinner, but you forgot utensils, so our meals got cold waiting. Before you headed off, Lynn ordered another beer and hot sauce. The beer came halfway through the meal and Lynn asked for hot sauce again. It never arrived.

I shook my head in disbelief. Shoney's Big Boy restaurants used a ten-step process that servers were required to follow. It simplified a server's work and was intended to satisfy the customer.

All those years ago, a daily patron paid me a dollar every day for a fifty-cent coffee. One client tipped five dollars for a six-dollar meal and said, "I've traveled all over the world, and that was the best service I've ever gotten." Shoney's secret shopper caught me conducting all ten steps in correct order. My Shoney's experience made me expect more from you, I realized.

The couple across the aisle had watched and listened. The man reared back in his chair and announced, "You've gotten lousy service." The woman leaned toward us. "She doesn't know where her bread is buttered." I shrugged.

Then, as you cleared our plates, Lynn ordered a third beer. You nodded.

After ten minutes of enjoying the sound of the surf, we gave up waiting, and asked for the check. While Lynn checked the bill to see if you had charged us for a third beer, I took time to explain why you would not get a good tip.

"We waited half-an-hour for you to take our order, my margarita came late, you forgot our utensils." Pointing to Lynn, I said, "He never got his hot sauce." Your eyes widened, then you dropped your head and nodded. "He never got the third beer." You looked up and frowned in confusion.

At that moment, Lynn called your attention to the tab. You argued that he had ordered three beers and he waved to the two bottles on the table you had served him.

You hung your head. "Lo siento!" *I'm sorry.* I glanced at the amount Lynn had laid down. "No cambio," no change.

You calculated the amount, then your face opened. Your first smile emerged. Your head bobbed. "Gracias, muchas gracias, señor!"

Lynn's tip surprised me, too. I prided myself in being a generous tipper, but my attitude had been prideful, ungracious, and ungrateful.

When you left, the man across the way admonished Lynn with raised eyebrows, "I don't tip for poor service."

Lynn said, "I tip to get good service next time."

Decades later, I still think about you. I wonder about what was going on that day as you passed our table, ignoring us. Was there a death in the family or a sick child at home that was your distraction?

What was it about Lynn and me that made us invisible or undesirable? Did our newfangled water bottles tell you we would not buy drinks and thereby reduce your tip? Something else? I will never know if the fact that you avoided us was about you or about us.

I learned a lesson from Lynn. Generosity comes with grace. So I offer you grace, grace, and grace, today and always.

Author's note: A letter to a stranger is a different genre of essay writing promoted by Colleen Kinder in her 2022 title, *Letter to a Stranger: Essays to the Ones Who Haunt Us.*

The Oppressed
Charlotte Wlodkowski

They cry out, but are ignored. I search my soul and ask why.

Their names are like no others: Running Fawn, Awena (meaning sunrise), Kanga (meaning black bird). They celebrate the spring equinox, while I patiently wait for the first robin.

Why do we recognize the Italian, Chinese, Polish, and other cultures but not the Native American? Why have the people of immigrants seamlessly blended into the fiber of our country, while Native American women still struggle to keep their identity? Worse yet, these females are shunned, as if they are not living, breathing, human beings.

Statistics report these women are two-and-a-half times more likely to experience violent crimes such as sexual assault, physical abuse, and homicide. Many go missing, never to be found. Murder is the third leading cause of their death. Any one of them could be my sister, aunt, or cousin. The worst atrocities are committed on their own reservations. In one state, only 116 cases were entered into the federal database from 5,712 reports of missing Native American women. Why? These women ask for help from local police, but little to no help is given.

The federal and state officials admit more than half of violent crimes aren't even investigated. Although tribal leaders govern their reservations, many have no authority to protect or take action for women who are abused. This is scandalous. It is neglect of the state and federal bureaucrats. The hurt and pain experienced by these women is magnified by the fact that law enforcement has abandoned them. Too many centuries have passed, and these Indigenous females are still suffering.

After being physically abused by my spouse, I sat with a friend in silence at a police department for almost an hour, just waiting to file a report. Only when the gravity of my situation hit me and I began to cry, did an officer recognize me. He never looked me in the eye, nor gave any sympathy. The officer didn't explain what my rights were, which gave me a feeling of helplessness. He asked questions and completed a form. My experience was worth only a form. My impression during the questioning was that he wanted this done and me to go away. In turn, I wanted to leave and be safe with my friend.

A day after, I was again surprised when, accompanied by a different officer, we went to my apartment to claim my personal belongings.

The officer asked my spouse permission to enter. This was degrading. I contributed to the upkeep of our living quarters. It further confirmed how unimportant I was.

Even after some forty years, I still remember the first blow. It was to the side of my face, but it was such a shock that I didn't feel anything. I found myself backing up, since he was approaching me to do more harm. I couldn't scream. I felt helpless, and I was. The blow caused a hairline fracture to my jaw, as my dentist told me. Afterwards, I was ashamed and in disbelief. How could someone who I loved, and proposed love for me, do such a brutal thing?

After that first incident, I was always fearful of saying or doing something he would deem unsuitable. Others find it difficult to understand why a woman would stay in an abusive situation. I made a commitment and wanted to be married. I, like many other women, was prone to believe we can fix things. Lastly, I thought it would never happen again, as he vowed. It took a total of three episodes before I escaped.

In a Native American home, the spouse is often the only breadwinner. Indigenous women have nowhere to flee. Their home and family are on reservations. Without support services, they have no choice but to stay where they are. This gives the abuser every opportunity to again commit violence.

Why do some men treat women as personal possessions and not as humans? Abusers tell us lies, criticize our every move, and give orders about whom we may talk to and where we may go. Out of fear, we begin to obey. The abuser often manipulates a woman into thinking she was the cause of the outrage. One day, I realized I was losing myself. I no longer lived in our world. I was a captive in his world.

Currently, there is a lack of justice for the victim and a lack of access of support services. Many women ask, who will protect me and my children if I leave? Repercussions are always a concern for women. It's a danger to relatives if they offer aid. Any aggression toward the abuser is immediately handled by the law. Why is there such a difference in treatment? The law should treat all people the same, but it does not.

Once I left my abusive spouse, I was stricken with fear. His livelihood was as a mechanic. Every time I intended to drive my car, I would first look at the tires and hope he didn't puncture any of them. As I turned the key to start my car, I prayed. It would take only a small missing part for me to be stranded. This would be an out-of-pocket expense I couldn't afford.

Being married only three years, there were no children involved, which made my break-up easier. It was both a blessing and a disappointment, as I remain childless. Because I was a recipient of abuse, I can attest that I will carry stories of tragedy and loss forever. It takes only a word or action to remind me of those terrible days. I identify more easily with those of us who have been abused.

We may have diverse backgrounds, come from unfamiliar cultures, and live in different areas, but we have the same outlook on life. I want these women to realize that whatever the circumstances, they can bring about a new and better life for themselves and their children. To help women make the change, I authored a book that offers them hope and courage. In the past, I have stepped in when I saw abuse happening and I encourage others to help those who are still in distress. We women need to take charge and show the abuser we will not let this happen again.

Mining for Gold
or A Tourist Guide to Aging
Ariela L. Zucker

> With mirth and laughter let old wrinkles come.
> — *William Shakespeare*

People say beauty is only skin deep. They also say *wrinkles should merely indicate where smiles have been.* (Mark Twain) It's a sign of wisdom earned through life experience. But in the same breath, they also say, iron out the wrinkles; let's get it right this time.

They call them the 'golden years' with a fleeting smile that flickers and then fades.

Golden indeed...

One can only wonder about the many words said in a futile attempt to shed a positive light on the unavoidable process of aging. I try to imagine aging as the final frontier (although less glamorous than circling the stars). I try to gather the energy required for a far-away journey. Going to space might be an elegant way to skirt old age by fooling time.

All this goes through my mind when I look at the foggy mirror in the early morning hours, or the harsher, bright neon light late at night. There is no way to pretend that it is not happening. The deepening lines that won't fade away, the puffy eyes, the thinning hair, they are here to stay.

This is the familiar me, yet unknown at the same time. I can either keep searching for the person I was, hoping to get a glimpse of her behind the new facial terrain. Or I can accept the developing proof and like the geographer I once was, gather the courage and my thirst for the road.

In my search for guidance, I discovered many journals and books—an abundance of information that any tourist to a foreign land can thrive on. Some of it is strictly informational, some overloaded with motivational mumbo-jumbo.

Still, no words can convey the entire vista. It is a foreign land that, as a traveler, I need to explore by myself. Listen to the language, observe the conduct, walk the terrain, and converse with the natives and other travelers. As the aging culture slowly reveals itself to me, I realize how many obstacles it presents, and how different the rewards are.

I recall one of my favorite books, Douglas Adams' *The Hitchhiker's Guide to the Galaxy*. How, with a sense of humor, it reveals a foreign terrain that on the surface lacked rhyme or reason. The language, scenery, and inhabitants unfamiliar and odd. The land of aging presents a different slew of challenges. The main one is the illusion of familiarity.

I can try to fool myself into believing that nothing has changed. It is still the same town where I have lived for seventeen years. The weather, with its whimsical behavior of snow and rain. The change of seasons and the return of familiar colors.

Familiar, but so different. What a baffling scenario.

Unlike traveling to a foreign land—I revoke my own analogy—I did not board a plane and find myself within a few hours in an unknown location. Aging is more like riding a slow train across the plains. Gradual changes, some not immediately observed, settle in the windows but never move on. Health changes, movement limitations, added medications, and a schedule filled with visits to health professionals. My attempts to minimize the changes, to pretend that they have no bearing on my daily life, have proven futile.

The land of aging is a continuous journey without a happy end. Who will be interested in this type of tale? Is it still possible to celebrate victories? Another year has passed; I am still here, still able to hold my own, my memory mostly intact. Those are not likely to be written down or used at family gatherings where photos will be taken or others presented.

When I follow the media portrayals of the very-old-specimen of the human race, it is with mixed feelings. This woman, who lived to be 103 years old, or this man, who is still conscious at the age of 105—they smile at the reporter from behind their lined faces and answer some nonsense questions about their secrets to longevity.

These are the journey's veterans, but the medals we honor them with always seem to me like superficial glitter. If we do not avert our eyes and look straight into theirs, we will see the deep tiredness, the heart, and the unspoken desire.

When the time comes, they say, do not stuff me in a hospital bed, or stick me with needles and false smiles.

Please, please, stop this train. I want to get off.

I'll walk by myself to the end of the trail.

Like an old Eskimo man or woman, I will turn my back and walk the ice to this alcove where utter quiet resides.

And, no, do not follow me, and I will not be back.

The land of aging—if I try to create an enticing ad for people to join, what would be the attractions I could offer? Unable to devise the cheerful tone that will tempt a tourist, I resort to what is already out there:

- Livable Communities for Aging Populations
- Finding Life in the Land of Alzheimer's
- The Ultimate Plan for Staying Young
- In the Land of Dementia
- A Light on Altered Land
- Older, Wiser, Fiercer
- Aging Backwards: Fast Track
- Younger You
- Healthy Aging
- Wise Aging
- Mindful Aging
- The Grace in Aging
- Redefining Aging

The messages seem to repeat. If anything, they come across as a travel advisory.

Level 1 — Blue – Exercise Normal Precautions.
Level 2 — Yellow – Exercise Increased Caution.
Level 3 — Orange – Reconsider Travel.
Level 4 — Red – Do Not Travel.

STANDING ALONE

INTERVIEW
Kathie Arcide

Remembered for the SCN Writing Extravaganza

It was the gunshot-blood splatter on the photographs that haunted me for years.

When my mother had finally had too much pain in her life, she drove into the mountains, laid out pictures of her daughters on the car seat, drank a gallon of wine, wrote messy goodbye notes…and finally, she gave up.

Those droplets of blood were on the fronts of my younger sisters' pictures…but on the back of mine, so I always assumed that me being a pregnant, unmarried teenager had thrown her back into terrible memories of her own experience of carrying me. I always assumed my birth represented the beginning of her long list of failed dreams. I assumed my mom was disappointed in me, even disgusted with me, so she couldn't look at my face at the end of her life.

> *In my therapy practice I use Psychodrama techniques; the short definition is acting out stories we carry in our heads about events and their meaning. While inside us, these stories are fact. But brought out into the light, mistaken assumptions about meaning can show up. This process can help us make new decisions about ourselves.*

A few years ago, when finishing up some therapy about my mom, I interviewed her in my own Psychodrama scene, during the last twenty minutes of her life. I played both of our parts in a detailed role reversal exercise. Acting as my mother, I listened to my tortured daughter's many questions.

Kathie asked, "Why did you choose to die rather than helping me keep my baby? How am I supposed to take care of my infant, *and* all my younger sisters? They're your children, not mine."

For many years, my internal-story answers from my mother were filled with resentment. I imagined her saying things like, "This serves you right. Now you'll know what it's like to have a baby ruin your life."

During this new, in-absentia "interview," when I asked my Mom why my photo had been turned face down, she said the exact words I had always imagined…"I just couldn't look at you." But now, putting myself fully in her shoes, *how* she said it was completely different.

"I just couldn't look at *you*." There was no disgust, only love, only sorrow.

Now I get that had she seen *my* face in those last moments, she could not have left me.

Now I see that in her lifelong, cumulative pain, she desperately needed relief.

Now I understand that my mother's final act had nothing to do with me. She truly believed she had no other choice.

TO THE MOTHERS OF UVALDE
Sharon L. Charde

The horrific shooting at Robb Elementary in Uvalde, Texas, has already been obscured by the January 6 hearings, the frightening drop in the stock market, the Russian capture of most of the Donbas region of Ukraine, and all the other bad news that crowds my inbox.

But it has not been eclipsed in my mind. I continue to feel intensely the throbbing bite at my soul these monstrous mass killings produce.

Because I know what it is to lose a child.

As do the mothers of Stoneman Douglas, Sandy Hook, and Columbine. Buffalo, Pulse, Ukraine, and yes, even Russia—they are mothers after all—how I imagine we are all thinking of you, Uvalde mothers, feeling with you, anguishing with you over the loss of our children.

Our lives have changed in ways we never could have imagined.

Some of us have long known these changes. Uvalde mothers, raw and stunned with sudden agony, you are just discovering how this assault on your existence will characterize your coming days, weeks, and months. You will soon find out who your real friends are. Some will back away from you, and you will be surprised. Your naked emotion is too hard for them to handle, it touches off reactions in them they are too frightened to touch.

Some of them will say appalling things to you, like "Only the good die young," "God needed another angel," "Well, at least you have another child," "Everything happens for a reason," "There are no accidents," "I know how you feel," and my personal favorite of all these dreadful clichés, "God never gives us more than we can handle."

Really?

Yet we go on, somehow, limping into a future empty of our child. Our lives, so ruthlessly sliced into "before" and "after," become too hard for others to comprehend.

Grief gets into our bloodstream, a partner for life.

Some imagine that we will return to the selves we were before the loss of our child and they relate to us in that way. Friends chatter about their children and grandchildren, showing us pictures on their phones, speaking of the graduations, proms, birthdays and weddings our dead child will never have. We attend some of these events, celebrating with friends and relatives, with quiet anguish an ever-present undercurrent in our hearts.

Somehow, some day, dear mothers of Uvalde, you will learn to carry your grief in a way that doesn't crush you daily. You will struggle to find the tool that will allow you to do that. It might be a garden, a scholarship fund in memory of your child, a crusade for gun rights, a community of fellow grievers, the comfort of religion or a renewed spiritual life, volunteering for a cause, starting again in a new home or area of the state or country.

It might be just the profound struggle to learn, day by day, how to be alive in your strange new world.

Your heart has been broken; your former life shattered. Respect that absolute new fact.

Tend your grief carefully as it is part of you now. Stay with it, get to know it, let yourself feel it fully. Try not to push it away, numb yourselves with alcohol or drugs, frantic activity, or all the other unhealthy panaceas so readily available in our crazy consumer culture. Attempts to silence it will only backfire, produce extra pain. Embracing your heartbreak keeps you connected to your lost child.

Do not listen to people who say, "You'll get over it." You won't.

But you will someday laugh again, though a current of loss and memory will always course beneath that laugh.

And in time, you will summon the strength to fully love your other children and your spouses. You will learn to work at keeping them from drowning in your grief, understanding that they need to mourn their own losses, that they may grieve differently from you.

And know it's possible to survive, even though you cannot now imagine how you will do that.

I have.

Dearest mothers of Uvalde, I'll be with you in spirit, a sister in sorrow, as you find your way.

ODE TO DEATH

You gave me no time-outs, dear death, yes
I called you dear, you heard correctly. Others
find you fearsome but I embrace you. No
way to stop being everything but what I
was to all the edges. No noticing anything
but what was right there, in front, in back,
underneath, on top of me. Restricted to your
greedy snare, I couldn't move, had no prayer
to pull me out, no *god wanted him* or *he's
another angel now,* to soothe. *Only the good
die young* left me comfortless, time hasn't
healed. I can still scratch the scab away, feel
your raw wound. Such purity, to feel only
pain. I don't blame you anymore, you happen
every day to everyone, why not my son?
Death, you've offered me a kind of peace.
I'm unable to return to the place I was
before you came. Separated from others
who don't know you yet, I stand alone.
You're too sad for me, people say. You give
me solitude. You give me singularity, a kind
of dignity I'd never have if not for you. Death,
your dowry has been paid, we're married now.

Previously published in *The Lakeville Journal,* June 22, 2022 (without the poem).
Poem from *Unhinged,* Blue Light Press, 2019, by Sharon Charde.

GENERATIONAL TRAUMA
Debra Dolan

I am a woman who has forgiven my mother for marrying my rapist. It took me nearly half a century, yet it has happened. Still feels somewhat repulsive when I see the words strung together, another aspect of my lived experience to overcome. My mother was never without decency or kindness. Over the years she has done a lot of nice things for me and I am grateful for so much. For most of my life, I was profoundly conflicted about our relationship. In the 1970s, my friends would comment that she was unlike the other mothers. She was sophisticated, well groomed and sexy. Hannah's German accent was exotic and she dressed to emphasize her legs.

I did not understand what was happening between Keith and me when I was young. I was embarrassed to try to explain to anyone at first because I wasn't sure what it was. I remember thinking, "Wait a minute, was that right?" Looking back, I thought the kissing, fondling, and genital exposure was because I was special and I had a father's affection. I don't recall Keith saying that we had secrets, but I was aware it only happened in private. It was extremely confusing because I also loved him.

One night he came into my room. He had been drinking and was breathing erratically. To this day I cannot stand the smell of beer on a man's breath. I instinctively knew that this experience with him would be different from the other times. I pretended I was asleep. I was wearing violet-colored baby doll pajamas and he pulled them down past my knees. Then, he penetrated me deeply with his fingers. It hurt very much. I recall a sensation of disassociation, of separating myself from what was happening in that traumatic moment, of being the bystander to, rather than the subject of, this attack.

The next morning my rage burst. I told my mother what happened. I had pushed my dresser against the door so no one could enter. I was crying. My mother was very upset. At a later point—it might have been a few days or a week—she told me that she had spoken to Keith and that what had happened would never happen again. And it did not. But the damage had already been done, the trust broken beyond repair. I became frightened of him. I did not want to be left alone with him. With my babysitting money, I bribed younger siblings, Christine and David, to stay home with me while Mom was at work, and when they would not, I attacked them. As soon as I was old enough, I left, and have not been back in decades.

Keith had been in my life since I was six years of age. My birth father abandoned my mother and us children three years earlier. Mom married Keith when I was a teenager. She married him in a civil ceremony at the courthouse months before she birthed a son, his first after three daughters.

It was not until my thirties that I understood that what Keith had done was rape, and that he had groomed me over time to gain my trust. A wrong had been committed against me, and no one stepped up to take responsibility. In addition to telling my mother, I told an older stepsibling and a teacher. No one responded with meaningful action. I was a child. The trust and security I relied upon in those most formative pre-pubescent years evaporated. I have worked very hard to regain them, alone and in my own way. I have learned that Keith died of natural causes in 2016 at the age of 92.

I know I am not a fairy-tale daughter, and Mom used to scare me when she would say in anger/frustration, "I hope you have a daughter just like you!" Ouch. It couldn't have been easy with three young children and being only 25-26 years of age herself. I think of this often. I wish I knew more about her. I always felt it was a form of cruelty when she would not reveal the "family story," answer my questions about my own childhood or father, or share photographs of me when young

I understand that Mother is deeply loved by my siblings, her eleven grandchildren and five great-grandchildren. I remember her making "doll cakes" for my birthday and helping me sew. I remember her loving afternoon matinees, and we would curl up on the couch making it fun to be home sick from school. Mom supported Brownies, dance (ballet and jazz), etiquette and swimming lessons, and always ensured we had lovely summer camping vacations and getaways at Thanksgiving in upstate New York. She was proud of my accomplishments, and was an attentive listener when I came home from school or a play date with a friend.

My mother was a young mother. She had me when she was a teenager. Although, years later, she made decisions in her own life that deeply affected my sense of self, and created much distance between us,

I owe her real gratitude for the happy early years we shared together as a family. It is very hard for me to accept that my mother married my molester. As I write this, I hurt so deeply, even though those events are over 45 years ago. I am profoundly conflicted about my relationship with my mother, always have been. I don't believe we will ever reconcile, although I have no doubt that she loves me very much. I also believe that she has suffered privately for her decision to stand by Keith when I came forward.

One of my favorite childhood stories, told by her, is how I would cling to my pet stuffed skunk (a gift from Uncle Dee?) with a tenacity bordering on desperate. I can still remember its charming, sweet, rubbery face. My mother told me that whenever it was taken from me to be cleaned, I would stand, sad and longing, in front of the washing machine waiting for the ordeal to conclude. I didn't want him to suffer. She used to love going to the laundromat so that she could use six or seven washers/dryers all at once. She always bought a women's magazine and Cherry Blossom chocolates.

I believe she has had a hard life. Her mother died when she was young and she immigrated to Canada with her workaholic absent father (due to the St. Lawrence Seaway) and three brothers—Karl, Horst and Dieter—without knowing English. Her teenage years certainly were not carefree. She told me once that she was terrified of her uncle, who had threatened her with a gun. I think something terrible happened to her and she never got over it. I understand that she told Keith she was ten years older than she actually was so that when they met, she was closer to his age than the nearly twenty years between them. In fact, she was very close in age with his three teenage daughters—Heather, Linda, and Nancy—when they met. This was confirmed to me many years later. I don't know much about their courtship or how they were introduced. As a child, it seemed sudden when we moved to his house in St. Catharine's. I believe I was six. In the early years, there was much volatility between them and her suitcases were in the hallway. Keith had not cleared his previous wife's belongings from the closet after her death. It took a few years to feel as if we belonged there. They told us kids they were married, yet did not marry until I was almost seventeen years of age. It was a private ceremony when she was pregnant with James.

I never had children. I wonder if I never wanted to be someone's "mother story."

This Too Shall Pass
Carolyn Foland

How often we say, "This too shall pass." In the face of difficult times, we remember—or are reminded—that this is not a permanent feeling. The comforting thought that nothing lasts forever. But then we also must recall that good times will pass, too.

The *Book of Common Prayer*, in the last service of the day—Compline—includes this prayer: "Keep watch…with those who work, or watch, or weep this night, and…over those who sleep. Tend the sick…give rest to the weary, bless the dying, soothe the suffering, pity the afflicted, shield the joyous.…"

"Shield the joyous." If reality is to shift, what better gift for children, for the innocent, for the vulnerable, for the unaware, for ourselves: the gift of time. A reprieve that forestalls a tragedy or waits for tomorrow's dawn to include sunshine, hope, and friends, along with whatever life carries.

It is said that without sorrow, we could not appreciate joy. While I acknowledge this, I also dread the piercing pain that comes from a telephone call, or a person who approaches you so carefully that you know they are going to say something that will hurt, sting, sorrow you. Some of us have given the bad news; some of us have received it. Sooner or later, most of us have experienced both. We learn as we receive, what helps and what does not.

My mother was seriously ill when I went away to university. Each time I was called to the phone in the basement of my dorm, or later at the apartment, when I heard my dad's voice, I expected to be told that she had died. It did not happen then. The news was brought by a friend when I was enjoying a picnic in the park a few years after I had graduated and was working. Grief had stalked me for years before it was released, yielding something that I had known was inevitable.

We should grab joy when we feel it, when it sneaks up and enwraps us in the soft pleasure of just being alive. Anne Lamott says that laughter is "carbonated holiness." No one exulting in pleasure pauses to announce, "This too shall pass." Dwelling in the present is a gift of the pleasurable intervals.

We do say those words during painful or even tedious times. When someone we love, doesn't love us back. When we sit in a dentist's chair. When we recover from surgery. When we have two choices, and neither will bring gladness to ourself or those around us. During longwinded speeches and bad plays. When we feel abandoned by friends, overwhelmed and alone.

Life rarely treats us as gently and respectfully as we think we deserve. It is the train without intermittent stops before our destination. When both our parents are dead, we are orphans for the rest of our lives. We watch our parents' siblings die and suddenly we and all our cousins are the "current" generation. And then our cousins leave us, too.

All life passes. The summers that lasted forever when we were children now go by with furious swiftness. The milestones that we set—when we could leave school, vote, have our first legal drink, get married, have children, get promoted, retire—all pass and we are left astonished by the truth of actuarial reckoning. The deadlines we ultimately face are not set by us.

A friend of mine who is a Catholic priest has an older mentor who has been slowly moving into the realm of dementia. My friend is in his seventies, with a travel schedule for retreats and speaking engagements that keeps him on planes and in airports a good bit of the time. He was feeling his age and wanting to cut back. He said to his mentor, "At times it's good for you to give up some things." His friend reflected, "And some things are taken from you."

There are metaphors for the intervals of life's experiences. The growth of springtime, the dying of fall and winter. The planting, then harvesting and plowing under. The beauty of a budding flower and the pale shades of its withering.

I always think of myself as I was when I was in my thirties and forties. When life still seemed endlessly stretched before me and anything—anything and everything—was ahead. "This too shall pass," I said, as I pushed through difficult times. But life is comprised of sadness and joy. It is a zero-sum game that we are in. There is a finite amount of life. And it all passes. Too quickly.

For all of us.

I'M AFRAID
Juliana Lightle

I'm afraid; I'm hungry; I'm cold.
I have no money.
No matter what make up I've used,
they know I'm indigenous,
a dirty Indian good for only one thing.

Tina disappeared last year.
Everyone knows what happens.
They do not even bother to look for First Nations women.
Women like me, worthless, don't matter.

Daily we disappear, used, beaten.
I don't want to be one of those disappeared women.
The shelter is not safe;
looks lovely but they just traffic
us to the miners and oil-field workers.

You go missing, no one cares.
You're lucky to even make the local papers.
There's no real work for women like me.
I'm afraid; I'm hungry; I'm cold.

I do not want to die.

Short Talk with Dorothy on Her Birthday
Margaret Dubay Mikus

(last night)

She did not feel like herself
she whispered into the dark
yet she sounded more like her voice
since the stroke, triggered
by cancer treatment probably
and by all the therapeutic drugs
in the years since the beginning.
She doesn't want to eat.
It is hard to swallow.
After nine years of struggle
we have arrived here yet
her husband, who has been a superhero
doing the impossible
caring for her at home
does all that needs to be done
alone.
His choice not to get help.
Yes, it is the pandemic still.
But she is there alone with him
and heading off the cliff
when she could be preparing
to let go and fly.
And I am the witness
to her suffering, struggling myself
not to drown.

Self-Empathy, Healthy Compassion, and Trees

Sandra Stanko

The trees were barren, their limbs creaking as they swayed gently in the crisp Western Pennsylvania January air. The brush was gray and brittle, dry leaves crunching under my feet. Where was the life? My own father's had just left this earth following a freakish choking accident from which he died not once but twice. Too much for one person. Not unlike my father now, this winter forest belied any life within and certainly any inherent wisdom. Most everything seemed dead.

A year earlier, my father's heart had worn out. He was having palpitations and then fainted. He needed an emergency pacemaker. A few weeks later, my own heart started to beat erratically; it would actually pause in its beating and then double-time beat to make up for the lost beat. This sensation felt like I had lost my breath and was choking. The ER doctor's diagnosis was premature ventricular contractions, or PVCs, a type of heart arrhythmia that is normal to have occasionally and which can be triggered by low electrolytes, stress, anxiety, caffeine, or a thyroid condition. And, strangely, even by empathy. My psychiatrist explained that on a subconscious level, I was likely mirroring my father's heart issues with my own, trying to unconsciously take some of his burdens onto me to alleviate his suffering. The truth was that it did none of that—it only made me scared and sick, with no relief to him.

Empathy can be said to be sharing the emotions of another. As I experienced firsthand with my father, scientists believe that the key to empathy may be the functioning of mirror neurons, the brain's neurotransmitters that can "mirror" the experiences of others. As in my case, the problems come when the person mirroring cannot differentiate between what is her own emotion and what is the emotion of someone else. While empathy is a useful evolutionary trait that can provide insights into how to help to relieve the sufferings of others, empathy untethered can be destructive, trigger a person's stress response, and lead to empathy fatigue. The result can be personally devastating. Empathy needs boundaries that begin with empathy for one's self.

Empathy - Boundaries = Increased Stress and Anxiety
Empathy + Boundaries = Self-Empathy and Healthy Compassion

Establishing boundaries is an expression of self-empathy and can transform personally destructive, stress-inducing empathy into expressions of healthy compassion. Looking to the trees can provide a model for healthy empathy. In her book *Finding the Mother Tree*, author Suzanne Simard explains how trees communicate through a complex underground network—dubbed the "Wood Wide Web"—in which mycorrhizal fungi live on the tree roots and are used by the trees to send messages to one another through chemicals that are identical to human brain transmitters. Moreover, Simard has found that a "mother tree" can recognize her own offspring and pass wisdom to her specific descendants while leaving other offspring to the care of their own respective mother trees. This form of compassion for their kin is created by a combination of neurally transmitted empathy, via the mycorrhizal fungi, within the boundaries the mother trees have established with their own kin.

We can follow the tree's model by embracing emotional mindfulness in setting personal boundaries. Like the tree roots, these boundaries establish a special type of personal shield, enabling virtual emotional osmosis by creating a selectively permeable membrane to control what passes through, rather than being unwittingly deluged by a flood of others' emotions.

Creating Healthy Boundaries

Although establishing a personal shield may sound like it is shutting others out and decreasing one's capacity for empathy, it is actually the opposite. Shielding, similar to osmosis, can block toxic energy, while enabling the flow of positive energy and the expression of healthy compassion in tandem with self-empathy. To build and maintain your shield, envision yourself surrounded by a white or pink bubble of light and take these suggestions from the trees:

1. **Be mindful of your current state and space.** Trees are aware of their surroundings. For example, some trees, such as poplars and birch, are genetically programmed to grow tall, but these trees will stay shorter when the tree canopy is crowded and the space to grow is limited. Similarly, your surroundings can profoundly affect your state of being, and can make you feel untethered, disoriented, and confined. Recognize your physical and emotional space in the present moment. Take a deep breath, get a drink of water, or engage in some other way with your senses to ground you.

2. **Find a safe place in nature.** Humans are energetic beings, and research is showing that trees emit similar types of electromagnetic energy. The difference, though, says Ora North, author of *I Don't Want to be an Empath Anymore*, is that natural energy is neutral and balancing; it does not self-impose itself on a person like human energy might do. So it can be helpful to retreat to nature as a safe place for re-energizing yourself and strengthening your personal shield. Just connecting with the earth by sitting in the grass or walking barefoot can be calming. Absorbing the tree's emitted phytoncides, or essential oils, and the negative ions emitted by dense forests, running water, and thunderstorms, has also been shown to relieve stress and anxiety.
3. **Decide what is acceptable for you in the moment and what is not.** In the forest, the ancient oak tree is not trying to impress the neighboring young maple sapling. People, however, often feel compelled to put others' needs before their own, which can trigger the stress response. This stress response can include not only *fight* and *flight*, says writer and life coach Dr. Martha Beck, but also *fawn*, where a person goes to extreme lengths to cater to the needs of others as a people pleaser. If you have this people-pleasing tendency, take a step back to acknowledge that you are enough just as you are. Focus on yourself and your needs rather than sacrificing your inner peace just to please someone else.
4. **Listen to inner wisdom and emotions without becoming overwhelmed.** Mother trees can be said to have developed inner wisdom that enables them to communicate with their kin and continue to proliferate. For a person, inner wisdom is a valuable teacher because it is a voice in tune with yourself, your needs, and your greater purpose. If you are feeling stressed or anxious, don't dismiss the feeling or become frustrated with yourself. Justine Froelker, author of *100 Devotions for Kids Dealing With Anxiety*, says that there is a difference between *feeling* emotions and *being* emotions. For example, you can *feel* anxious in a way separate from yourself as opposed to *being* anxious, where you invite the emotion into your inner being. The former can provide you with valuable insight into your emotional triggers, while the latter can be emotionally overwhelming. Listen to what you are feeling and sensing while maintaining some distance from the emotion.

Your emotions can be your superpower, but they do not have to overpower you.

Self-Empathy in the Forest

As I walked in the forest following my father's death, I looked beyond the apparent barrenness. The Pennsylvania state tree, the eastern hemlock, remained evergreen with its soft, tiny green needles. The Japanese pachysandra, devoid of the tiny white flowers it would sprout in the spring, had its bright evergreen serrated leaves spread across the forest floor. And the Pennsylvania state flower, the mountain laurel, which blooms with a compact pink flower in the spring, had stayed evergreen in winter with its broad green leaves. Two of the former are my namesakes, Sandra Laurel. And, of course, below my feet, the Wood Wide Web was active, fungal synapses firing and mother trees creating boundaries and showing compassion within and among their kin. As the winter breeze enveloped me, I envisioned my protective shield, white with ribbons of evergreen reflecting my namesakes. I remembered my father. I stepped forward into the trees with self-empathy…and healthy compassion.

VETERANS DAY AT THE VETERANS MEMORIAL
Pamela Stockwell

She stood against the glowing
Black marble
Where names are all that remained
Of young men's dreams
No trace here
Of mud
And steaming jungles
And terror
And grief
Unless you see it in your own face
Reflected darkly
On a bright November day

She stood against the marble
She herself a living monument
Her flesh marked by war
Deeply etched
But not so deep
As the scars of her soul

We knew her as a child
Fleeing senseless destruction
Her spirit as vulnerable
As her naked body
As she ran toward the camera
That caught her agony
And flung it out into the world

Her hair is black now
As it was then
Ebony, like the stone behind her
Her eyes dark
Cryptic
Delphic
Until she smiled
At the nation that had scorched her
Body and soul
And proved that
Forgiveness is a gift
That is not, after all,
Beyond our reach

CRACKS THAT NEED HEALING
Jo Virgil

As I walk along the Violet Crown trail,
Just below my feet and deep underground
Limestone rocks keep the earth steady, firm, solid.
Trees learn to wind their roots around the stones,
Or maybe through them.

The rocks have cracks, have holes, have tiny caverns.
The aquifer runs through the cracks,
Seeping water from here to there, twisting and winding,
Sinking deeper, then finding a cliff and falling, falling,
Into a river, becoming one.

So are our hearts sometimes—firm and steady,
Until one day a crack forms, and the tears seep through it,
Twisting and winding, sinking deeper, falling, falling.
But then all that love and compassion that is in our heart
Finds its way out, lets the tears evaporate into the sky.

And our heart, our love, our trust, becomes steady, firm, solid,
And once again, we find ourselves peacefully flowing
Into all that is or ever will be.

Through Her Eyes
Ariela L. Zucker

She fell out of love
and the reasons are many,
she fell away from love
perhaps for geographical reasons.

When she bares the story
her eyes shine with unshed emotions.
When she looks for compassion in her
friends' eyes they deliberate.

Fell out of love?
Hmm, what really happened?
They prod with persistence, seek
for what they call…the true story.

Was it a change of heart,
a disappointment in the physical act
or perhaps words that crumbled
in a heap of loose gravel.

Melody of feelings, she tries to explain,
create orchestrated delicate notes
hemmed with care. Hues that highlight
soft wraps of a weave tailored with precision.
The skin that touches cell against cell can
turn nonverbal messages into epic tales.

And when the music screeches,
the touch turns dry. Then you fall out of love,
and what hurts the most is
when you remember how good it was.

EXPLORING THE MYSTERY

ANCESTRY SURPRISE
Patricia Daly

The popularity of DNA testing has, for many people, provided a lot more information than they ever expected or wanted to learn. In my family, a secret was revealed that no one saw coming. My brother's DNA test showed us that we did not have the same father, although we grew up in the same home and our parents were married to each other until their deaths. Both of us were dumbfounded by the data.

There we were, I in my seventies and he in his sixties, trying to make sense of the news. He and I were mutually confused, but he more so because he was dealing with the reality that the man who raised him was not his biological father. My own DNA information, obtained at least five years earlier, showed no mysteries whatsoever. Neither of us expected anything different from his results. But then it happened: the bottom fell out and we were left with questions and a quest.

The DNA report provided no clues about my brother's father. It was the absence of any mutual paternal relatives between our Ancestry matches that started the questions, as well as the statement that he was 44% Italian. There is not a drop of Italian blood in either my mother's or my father's Irish ancestry. But here is my brother, inexplicably 44% Italian.

My brother's driving question was, "Who then is this man who is my father?" My driving question was different. Now faced with the fact that my mother gave birth to another man's child while she was married to my father, I was driven to ask, "Who then is this woman who is my mother?"

My brother was on a mission of discovery of his father. My mission was one of trying to understand my mother.

He probably would not have found his father at all except for a last name in his matches that he asked me about. "Does the name L**** mean anything to you?" I froze as chills spread over my arms. "Yes," I responded, with deep sorrow. At that moment I knew who his father probably was.

Fifty years earlier, my first job was with the same organization where my mother had worked through the 1950s. When I started working there, seven years after she left to be a stay-at-home mom to me and her new baby, I worked with many of the same people she had, including her former boss, Mr. L. That was the clue my brother needed to begin his dogged pursuit.

I felt sympathy for him. He was an emotional wreck. Although my brother was able to successfully track down his biological extended family, he discovered his father already had been dead for twenty years, as was my mother, by then. Family members he identified were the grandchildren and great-grandchildren of the man who fathered him, and they were not interested in this sixty-year-old guy claiming to be the love child of their great-grandfather.

That was the saddest part of all—the deep feeling of rejection my brother experienced from newfound kin he wanted to meet but who simply didn't care. It was a double whammy for him. First, he realizes he has no blood relationship to a lifetime of grandparents, aunts, uncles and cousins he called family, then secondly, he is rejected by the people he is indeed related to by blood.

He was tortured by the question of why our mother had not told him. They were extremely close. He had not married and had lived with her until her death, when he was almost 40. My guess is that mom saw no benefit in telling him. During her lifetime there was no DNA testing, no Ancestry, no 23andMe. What would be the point of sharing her secret, when life had turned out okay the way it was? She took her secret to the grave for twenty years.

My questions for my mother, however, go further than "why didn't you tell me?" My mental probing asked when, where, and what, as in "WTF, Mom?"

Once I got beyond the obvious facts that included an affair and a pregnancy, I wanted to know more.

Was it a one-night stand, or an ongoing affair?

Was she in love with him, or was it exclusively a sexual attraction?

Was her marriage so unhappy that she reached out to another man for love and appreciation?

I know that my mother wanted to have more children after I was born, because she told me so. But she didn't get pregnant, not until my brother came along ten years after me. Maybe she thought she couldn't get pregnant. The speculation and questions go on and on without answers.

I do not know the depth of her marital unhappiness or what she had to cope with in her life with my father. Did she feel trapped? Did she long for a different life, one with the father of her son? I wonder and I feel sadness for her. There is so little I know about her personal history.

I'm not going to judge her one way or the other for her choices. I can't even make myself say she "should have" told my brother of his biological father, because I don't know the circumstances of her relationship with her lover, or if there was even a conversation between them about the child they shared. Because mom had a serious alcohol problem, I don't even know if she knew what happened.

A lot of socializing and partying went on in the '50s, particularly where my parents worked. It's easy to imagine alcohol-fueled coupling among co-workers.

Now that I'm in my seventies, my recollections of my mother's life, her marriage, her affair, and her relationship with her only son, are all seen in a new perspective. I perceive her life differently than I did at any other time in my life. Everything has shifted. This revelation has led me to try to understand her better as a woman and mother, perhaps a very unhappy one.

My mother and I were quite different persons, but even the personality and generational differences contain common connections between us that enable me to want to walk in her shoes for a time. Although the situation is something I never imagined, I'm not angry or disgusted by what happened. I, too, am an imperfect mother with faults and failures on my ledger.

Aging and the passing of time can mellow our judgments of our parents. If you're lucky, your perspective leans toward being less critical of the parent who is just as human as you are.

If you're lucky, you come away from difficult or painful memories released from the burden of anger or vindictive intention.

And if you're very lucky, you receive the gift of insight, or at the very least, the desire to understand what happened that led to the unfortunate and unintended.

The ability to see through the eyes of another, and even forgive, is a blessed moment that frees both you and them. That's what empathy can do.

Rethinking Marriage
Kathryn Haueisen

I have several grandchildren who are living with significant others but without a wedding date on the calendar. My options are to accept their choices or risk losing them from my life. To have empathy for them, I am faced with rethinking many assumptions I've held about marriage.

My parents were married until my father died, as were their parents before them. There are two conflicting stories about my grandfather's sister. One version claims she was stood up at the altar. The other version claims she was divorced, back in the early 1900s, when divorce was rare and shame for divorced people was common. Recently, I came upon an old photo labeled "Carrie and her husband." Evidently, she was married long enough for someone to capture them together. I suppose the tale of being jilted went over better than being divorced in a family that has perfected keeping embarrassing information hidden.

My mother's brother divorced when I was a young girl. Wife number two was a frequent part of my teen years. When she died, wife number three appeared on the scene, but by then I had started my own family in another city.

When my best high school friend announced she was getting a divorce, I was stunned. She was the first personal acquaintance of my own age to divorce. Over time the number of divorces among family and close friends steadily grew. It was like watching the spread of some sort of societal disease that apparently had no cure.

Being of the Protestant faith, I thought of marriage as a sort of minor sacrament. I presumed the "until death do us part" vows were non-negotiable. Though I tried not to judge those who did not live up to that standard, I did sometimes wonder if they had really tried hard enough. Then I was the one going through a divorce. For many months, I cringed when checking off "divorced" as the honest response to my marital status. Thirty years into our marriage things shifted. Some changes were obvious. Our children were grown and gone, and jobs took us to a new community where at first, we knew no one except one another.

Multiple sessions of marriage counseling did not convince my husband we should try to get to the bottom of whatever the problem was, and keep going. I reluctantly accepted my fate when the counselor asked, "Do you want to stay married to someone who doesn't want to be married to you?"

No, of course not. I wanted him to still want to be married to me. He did not. He was an unhappy man, and concluded I was the source of that unhappiness. There was nothing more to do but release him. It took years to reassemble the shattered pieces of my life. Writing a novel about the experience provided a significant portion of the recovery. What started as a personal journal turned into *Asunder*, a novel about divorce and recovery, complete with an appendix about the role of marriage in society through the centuries and what the Bible really teaches about divorce. There's plenty of grace to be found in scripture if you know where and how to look.

Six years later, I married again. I shouldn't have done so, at least not to the man I married. I attributed the warning signs to dating for the first time since living in a college dorm room. We traveled well together, but we did not live well together. When his own circle of friends started confirming what my family and friends had been pointing out, I listened. I filed for divorce and this time I was the one telling the counselor I was sure that is what I wanted.

I've had to seriously rethink my assumptions about marriage. It appears to me society as a whole is reconsidering the purpose and role of marriage in modern life. A stable, mutually beneficial marriage is a wondrous situation. I maintain it is also the best environment for raising children. David Brooks published "The Nuclear Family was a Mistake" in *The Atlantic* (March 2020). He wrote, "The family structure we've held up as the cultural ideal for the past half-century has been a catastrophe for many. It's time to figure out better ways to live together."

As we watch the hard-won rights for women being taken away, I think marriage is still the wisest course of action for women of childbearing age involved in a relationship that could lead to pregnancy. Birth control helps, but it is not 100% reliable. I think both a mother and father are best protected from future legal and financial challenges if there is a marriage certificate binding them to one another and their children.

However, staying in an unstable or non-nurturing marriage can be torture. When one person does most of the giving while the other receives the bulk of the benefiting, the relationship erodes to the point there is little left to salvage. Abuse, addiction, or adultery seem like adequate reasons to end a marriage, unless there is true repentance combined with changed behavior. Even when these are not factors, living in a non-nurturing relationship can feel like death by a thousand insults, combined with failure to thrive due to neglect and criticism.

We have overemphasized the romantic aspects of marriage, establishing expectations no two mere mortals could ever meet. Until a couple of hundred years ago, love had very little to do with marriage. "Traditional marriage" is a relative term, depending on what culture one is discussing. For centuries marriage brought two tribes or nations together, promoting enhanced wealth and prosperity for each. Marriages were arranged, with each family providing one of the two marriage partners.

The teaching about marriage as one man and one woman committing to one another for life has already been challenged legally in granting marriage licenses to same-gender couples. Alvin Toffler predicted in his 1970 *Future Shock* that modern marriage would consist of "serial monogamy." Dr. Clifford Sager, director of family psychiatry at the Jewish Board of Family and Children's Services in New York, confirmed what Toffler predicted. Andree Brooks quoted him in her 1985 *New York Times* article. "A generation or two ago you entered a marriage and you stayed with it for better or worse. Today we are seeing much more short-term bonding, with an increasing number of men and women going through serial marriages."

Is this good? Bad? Irrelevant? How do we build a stable society on shifting sands of family commitments? How can we structure a world in which every person born lives in dignity from birth to death?

Some use scripture as a weapon to pressure people into submitting to their version of family values. Scripture references at least several variations of marriage: patriarchy, matriarchy, polygamy, monogamy, marriage between cousins, exogamy, and patriarchy plus assorted concubines.

Marriage norms have shifted. We no longer shame women who are with child without a marriage license. We do a very poor job of helping them, but we no longer put scarlet "A's" on them. Home duties once typically done by housewives are now easily contracted out to a wide variety of pick-up and drop-off services. Few modern couples postpone sex until their wedding, eliminating marriage as the threshold to an active sex life.

Has marriage become obsolete? Perhaps we could do more to stabilize society if we focused on providing basic services for people, regardless of marital status. As a society we can do much more to support those rearing the next generation. What if we worried less about how consenting adults choose to live, and focused more on providing all adults with a livable wage, a safe environment, and adequate health care, regardless of marital status. How can we structure society so that every single man, woman, and child is part of a small network of caring people who help him or her buffer the inevitable storms of life?

What if we thought about marriage the way we think about careers? When one career is no longer suitable, people seek out another one. Perhaps we have evolved to the point where one relationship is not adequate to cover today's many decades of adult life. I wonder how society might best support people before, during, and after marriage—as well as couples who opt not to wed but still commit themselves to each other.

MY SON'S EYES
Christy-Holly Piszkiewicz

"Mama, why are you so sad?" my little Steven asked as I walked into his room. As he put his 5-year-old hand on my face, I felt my heart go lighter. There was a sparkle in his clear blue eyes, yet they also held an empathetic concern.

I was so surprised. I had thought I was doing well in hiding my grief from my children. But had he heard me crying or felt my depression?

I lost a four-month pregnancy just a few weeks before. Shaking my head, I realized, "No, it's ten weeks." The baby had died in utero. Every time I thought I could handle this, the sadness and emptiness seemed to overtake my mind.

I bent over to cuddle my second-born, and asked, "What do you mean, my sweetheart?"

"Are you sad that we don't have our new baby anymore?" he asked with delicate kindness. How did he get so wise, so consoling at his young age?

"Well, yes," I stumbled, picking my words very carefully. "But, Honey, you know God gave us you and your sister to be our family.

We love you." He put his fingers on my lips and stopped me from talking.

"I know, Mama," Steven said as he held his fingers tighter on my lips, "I am going to pray to God and ask him to send us another baby. Then you'll be fine."

I kissed that angelic face goodnight. "I'll talk to him," he mumbled sleepily.

I went downstairs with such a light heart, and nine months later, we welcomed Martin Simon to our family.

Martin, the brother Steven had prayed for.

Two Rivers Flowing
Janet Grace Riehl

Boasa remembered me. I had lived in his village a year previously, learning to speak his language and live graciously in his culture, the first outsider to ever live in Makalamabedi, the place where the two rivers meet.

Boasa not only remembered me, he knew me. His hands lightly encircled and supported mine as he took the pulse of my soul, all the while smiling and chatting in Setswana. I knew he knew me by the fleeting cloud of sadness that wrinkled his broad face between the glimmer and shadow of his dark eyes.

I'd never connected with anyone as quickly and completely as I did with Boasa, Makalamabedi's herbal doctor. Villagers went to him for any sickness or problem. You would be hard-pressed to discover an ailment of man or beast that Boasa had not treated. He had performed ceremonies for fevers and rashes, infertility and infidelity, the birth of a two-headed calf. I wondered what he could do for a half-souled woman.

What Boasa knew shimmered below the surface of our conversation as he searched out who and what I was. My palm in his, he sifted through the history of my life, gathering information for his healing work. Only when his twin brother Benjamin called us to dinner did he release my hand.

After eating, Boasa returned to his compound, slipping through the hoof-and-mouth disease control cordon. The fence, erected to protect

Botswana's precious cattle from the dreaded disease, ran the length of Botswana and divided Makalamabedi. Still, at designated points along the fence, people could pass through. The two sides were not isolated from each other, just divided. When Boasa departed, Benjamin led me to the Galatian Apostle Church, where he ministered nightly.

I sat waiting inside the church as small groups filtered in to swell the congregation. Each moved naturally to the benches on their proper side of the room, left or right, male or female. Lit by one lonely lantern, their shadows quivered on the walls of the sanctuary.

When we had walked together to the newly whitewashed and thatched church, Benjamin and I had been friends and equals. But now, standing at the front of the church behind the altar table elevated on a homemade dais, Benjamin shifted like quicksilver into God's messenger.

Attired in a red-sashed white robe, muscles lightly flexing beneath the cloth, he lit the altar candle and began his staccato Setswana chant. His shadow loomed behind him. As the sermon gained momentum and volume, his spittle flew toward us, arcing in the dusty lamplight.

"Children of God," Benjamin intoned, "we have a friend from across the sea with us tonight. She does not feel well."

As if on cue, alarmingly, I began to feel faint in the crush of bodies. A woman slipped her arms around my waist, and we shuffled outside. I slid down to the cool sand and rested my head on her ample lap. The moon sharply silhouetted the broad Marula trees and the cattle moving restlessly in their kraals.

Boasa emerged from the shadows. "Come," he said and led us toward the place of drums and singing on the far side of the quarantine divide. A fire, cupped by rocks and nestled in the sand floor, lit the inside of a mud hut. Boasa made a comfortable pallet for me by the fire, invited me to lie down, and covered me with an impala skin.

Drums beat; men and women sang, clapped, and danced in a circle around the fire. Boasa threw herbs into the flames, then came to lay his hands on my head and stomach. I understood no words of this chant, which prayed to spirits different from those Benjamin had invoked at the Galatian Apostle Church.

My eyes rolled up to the top of my head, and my body jerked violently. Part of me moved into a state of suspension while another prayed that I could trust this healer. Boasa's hands swooped over my body, sweeping away whatever malevolent influences might lurk there. My body sighed deeply and relaxed into a trance.

The chanting, drumming, and singing continued until the fire died down. Then Boasa settled next to me and lightly snapped his fingers beside my left ear. Gently, he guided me to sit and then to stand. "Go home to bed," he advised. "You are wobbly now, but by morning you will be fine."

When he squeezed my palm, I knew it would be so.

Truth Or Lie
Marlene B. Samuels

Regardless of just how much most of us, in this modern era, believe we know, the events of World War II and the acts of Hitler, specifically the brutality and inhumanity, linger in surprising and often unexpected ways. And no matter what we think we might know about our parents—those people who raised us, nurtured us and taught us not only life's most important lessons but everything we must hold sacred as well—shocking truths do continue to surface.

It's these truths that alter our perceptions of our parents and especially how we've come to our own understanding of the world at large. In the long run, what we believe about those people we've called Mom and Dad, trickles down the generational chain. Ultimately, our perceptions of our parents influence the ways in which we convey our own truth to our own children. I learned the truth about Sara, my mother, not many years ago—five at the most. It was at that time that I learned she had created an alternative reality about her past entirely for my benefit.

How honest are we with our children? That question was inspired by my mother's experiences during the Holocaust. The matter of parental honesty provides the much-needed opportunity to reassess the diverse ways in which we hope to protect our children. In thinking about childhood's perceptions, one frequently overlooked benefit for most of us is that when we are young children, our worlds often are limited, secular and secluded. The everyday life of childhood is but a small sliver that represents what we are certain is the world at large. As a result, it feeds the false perception that all families are just like our own.

In our adult lives as parents, how do we decide just what and how much of our pasts we will share with our children? How truthful we can be? Because how we decide is influenced in subtle ways by another question: what do we really know of our own parents' lives and of their truthfulness with us?

When she was a child, the girl asked periodically, "Mom, what happened to your breast?" She became ever more persistent as she began to mature and was gaining a natural awareness of her own female attributes.

"I was in Ravensbrück Concentration Camp. Your Aunt Esther and I, along with two other girls from my barracks, were sent to unload crates of food from a barge," she explained. "Two girls created a distraction while Esther and I stole some vegetables we stuffed into our shoes. The S.S. guards caught me." Her mother answered, each time without the slightest variation. "They beat me viciously. Dorothea Bintz—the most sadistic S.S. Guard of them all—got me right across my left breast with a pry-bar. She hit me so hard that it severed my nipple and part of that breast."

Decades passed. Her mother died far too young, her brutal truths buried with her. The girl, now about the same age as her mother was when she died, went to visit her brother in California. He was four years older than she and when they were growing up, he'd always been their mother's confidante. The girl always envied their special relationship.

"You know about Mom, right?" he asked her one evening during their visit.

"What, exactly, about Mom are you referring to? What is it you think I'm supposed to know about her?" she asked him.

"That she had been experimented on in the camps. That's the reason she was missing part of her left breast. You didn't ever wonder about that?"

The girl gasped. "I don't believe it! If that's true then why didn't I ever hear about it?"

"Maybe she didn't want you to know," her brother said. "Why else do you think she was so deformed? I'm curious about exactly what she did tell you happened to her?"

"That she was beaten by that sadistic S.S. Guard, Dorothea Bintz. That she had caught mom stealing food when the women inmates were unloading a supply barge."

"You do realize Mom lied to you, right?" he asked.

At once, the girl felt sick to her stomach, as though she might vomit. She was simultaneously shocked and devastated by the idea that their mother had lied to her about something so significant. But then, her feelings of anger began to erupt. She was furious that her mother had actually lied to her for so many years. "Why would Mom have told me such a detailed and elaborate lie for my entire life?" She struggled to hold her tears and anger in check. "I feel so utterly betrayed!" she confessed to her brother.

He remained quiet for a few minutes while he considered the most significant motivation for their mother's decision about how much to share and how truthful to be. He was enveloped by a calmness with which the girl was wholly unfamiliar.

"I have three children and you have two, right?" he asked, his voice slow and soothing. "So what would you have told your own kids if you had endured such inhumanity, the unbelievable atrocities that Mom did? Do you think, for one second, you would have told them the truth?"

"Never! Not in a million years!" she said, recognizing yet another feeling that was emerging—new understanding.

JUST IN TIME
Elena Schwolsky

Driving through unfamiliar yellow-brown hills dotted with subdivisions and strip malls, I grip the steering wheel so tightly my fingers ache. My anxiety about seeing my mother for the first time in months has joined with my worry about getting lost. The Flatiron Mountains, majestic and distant, appear first in front of me, then on one side or the other no matter which way I turn. But I am distracted from the beauty of the landscape by thoughts of my mother and our conflicted relationship. I wonder how I will navigate this new chapter in our lives.

Finally, I arrive at The Reserve, my mother's new home, the place my brother calls her *storage unit*. "Make sure there's no one near the door waiting to escape when you open it," he had warned that morning. He and his wife have been looking out for my mom since we moved her here a year ago, when her dementia had progressed to the point that she needed the safety of a locked facility. "Just in time," we reassure one another when doubt overwhelms us.

On the other side of the door, a small nurses' station opens onto a carpeted hallway dotted with people, many bent over in wheelchairs with only the tops of their heads showing. A woman in blue overalls paces back and forth with a baby doll in her arms.

"I'm Ruby's daughter, visiting from New York," I declare to one of the nurses at the desk. "How nice!" she says, and points me to a room down the hall.

The activity room is lit by sunlight filtering in through flowered curtains. Comfortable armchairs hug the walls. From one of these chairs, a staff member is reading a children's story in a loud animated voice. My eyes nervously scan the room. Where is my mother? I have prepared myself for the fact that she won't know me, but now I'm unable to pick her out from this crowd of vacant faces.

Finally, by process of elimination, I spot her. Her white hair is longer than it has been in years, hanging straight over her collar. She is seated in a wheelchair, her head thrown back, her hands picking at a black vinyl cushion that has been placed across her lap to restrain her. My mother, whose sharp glances could bore right through to my core during all the stormy years of our pre-Alzheimer's relationship, stares beyond me as I approach her chair and kneel beside her.

"Hi Mom," I begin tentatively. "It's Elena, your daughter. I'm here to visit with you." I hold her hand, which is hot and dry and covered with purplish blotches.

"Who?" she says, turning away from me. Her voice is a croak and it's clear she has no idea who I am. I remember how invisible I often felt in her presence and, for a moment, wonder why I have come.

All the childhood years of harsh criticism and alcohol-fueled mood swings left me with wounds I've worked hard to heal. As an adult, I've kept my distance and protected my own children from a grandmother I feared would hurt them, too. Now, in her last years, my mother is trapped in a dense fog. The effects of dementia, depression, and years of drinking twist through her days like a hopelessly snarled skein of colored yarn. I am trying to be a dutiful daughter, but I am caught between compassion and rage. Which will show up on this visit?

I go every day to help my mom with lunch. In the dining room of carpeted floors, dark flowered valances at the windows, and upholstered chairs with curved wooden arms, aides come around with large terrycloth bibs, which they fasten around each neck. At our table, Gracie is hunched in the chair across from us, chewing on a corner of her bib; Helen is rapidly eating everything on her plate with her fingers; and Bill is making public service announcements in a loud monotone.

My mother occasionally joins in the activity around the room by starting a conversation of her own. "Hello," she says with authority to the ceiling. "I certainly think so, don't you?" Sometimes she withdraws completely, squeezing her eyes shut, sealing her lips tight—refusing my offering of pureed meat and mashed potatoes, refusing even to acknowledge my presence beside her. One day, after one too many gentle urgings to eat just one more spoonful, my mother surprises me by opening her eyes and looking right at me. "You don't know my ups and downs in this fucking place," she says in the familiar voice that used to send me into hiding.

Everything feels strange to me here. The sky stretches like a huge blue tarp above my head, and I feel myself growing smaller each time I step out into the bigness of it all. On my morning drive to the nursing home, tumbleweeds roll across the road and prairie dogs pop up from holes in the fields. "It's okay, you'll be okay," I reassure myself aloud. Even my voice feels changed—high and tight in my throat. I am not myself here, and my mother is no longer herself. Will we find, in this new terrain, a different way of shaping our lives together?

When I arrive at The Reserve on the last day of my visit, I take deep breaths, give the door a push and enter, scanning the hallway and the activity room for her gaunt and fragile face.

Grief and regret form a lump in my throat; I can barely swallow. As I make my way down the hall, the memory of a painful struggle that unfolded between us a year earlier clings to me.

My mother had been stretched out on the couch in her small, assisted living apartment.

"Let's get you out of these pants and into some clean clothes, Ma." I gently tugged at one leg. She grabbed at the pants and shook her head no.

I managed to pull my mother's pants down around her ankles. The sight of her pale skinny legs, dotted with bruises from forgotten bumps and falls, was heartbreaking. She pulled her legs up to her chin and rested her head on her knees.

"I'm fine like this. Give me back my damn pants."

But I was already busy in her closet selecting an "outfit." In her heyday, my mother wore flowing colorful caftans and exotic jewelry. I remembered watching in awe as she readied herself for an evening out—brushing on rouge, mascara, and deep red lipstick. Ruby had style and flair, but she felt as far away from me then as she was as a frail old woman, smelling of dried urine, hanging onto her pants for dear life.

For the next ten minutes, I forced us into an excruciating battle of wills, a tug of war between mother and daughter, until my mother was curled into a quivering ball.

"Look, I don't care what you wear, but you are going to change out of those goddamned pants and put on something clean," I thundered, standing over her and shaking my fist. She began to whimper, then to cry in big gulping sobs punctuated with "please, please." I saw us then, in my mind's eye—my wrath, her fear and helplessness. In that moment, I made a choice. I called for a meal to be sent up, covered her with a soft red-plaid blanket, and we sat eating our roast chicken and watching a football game on T.V. Since that day, I have felt myself slowly letting go of the corrosive anger that has been my constant companion—I will not be *that* daughter.

"I love you, Mom," I say when I find her—words that rarely passed my lips in all our long and tangled life together—and bend to kiss her forehead.

"You're a good girl," she says, with the flicker of a smile parting her dry, chapped lips. Perhaps in some dim recess of her failing mind, she does know who I am and what I yearn for.

"You're a good, good girl," she says looking right at me.

And the words float through the distance between us, landing with a soft thud in a hollow place in my chest.

THROUGH MY MOTHER'S EYES
Connie Spittler

For years, I cared for my mother as she battled mental illness. She insisted on living alone, gripping her independence as tightly as she clung to her rosary beads. If she took her meds, she was fine, but when she felt better, she thought pills were no longer necessary. Once pills phased out, her cycle of mental torture returned. Mom's stories about the situations that occurred were unusual enough for me to try checking her in for observation. When she refused admittance, my only legal choice was for the court to have her declared insane. She looked me straight in the eye and said, "You wouldn't dare."

And she was right.

To try to understand her world, I wrote a story from her perspective, using her words from our conversations about the life she endured. In fact, the writing helped.

THE SORROWFUL MYSTERIES

Margaret's aluminum trailer sucked up the Arizona sunrays. She wiped her forehead as the steadily released heat invaded her ninety-year-old body. She knew it was time to pray her rosary. "My life is filled with heavy baskets of worries, like laundry," she thought. "My job is to smooth out each worry, fold the corners in to make them round as a doily, then turn each one into a prayer."

Enveloped in humidity, she began, "First Sorrowful Mystery." The shape of every bead comforted her, as she said each Hail Mary out loud, over and again, the passage of five decades that formed the rosary's circle.

"Hail Mary, full of grace," rolled from her tongue as the heat streamed in the open window. "I'll close it later," she thought as the roundness of beads began to ease her mind.

After Margaret promised the doctor she'd take her medication, he agreed she could try staying at home with regular daughter check-ins, an unplugged stove, and a microwave that would make Meals on Wheels unnecessary, but available.

"I can cook that way," Margaret told him. "I'll make oatmeal for breakfast, warm up TV dinners with vegetables and sometimes frozen pizzas as a treat. I'll eat the stews and soups my daughter brings over and swallow a vitamin for dessert."

Margaret smiled to herself at the way she'd convinced the doctor and then moved on with her praying. "Hail Mary," she continued. Each word soothed her soul, anointing her body with prayers as sweet as the rose fragrance that filled the warm trailer air.

When she reached the tenth bead marker, she pushed on, "Second Sorrowful Mystery."

Her fingers pulled and tugged along the beads as she intoned the words, like tightly wound flower buds growing within her chest. Her tugging at the rosary chains often broke the circle of beads. She wondered why rosary makers couldn't find wire strong enough to hold the prayers she set free, but she always saved the pieces, resurrecting them with bits of string. Her mind turned to the poison in her food. Lately, she could taste the bitterness. On those days, she didn't eat, just sipped slowly from a jelly glass filled with milk. "If babies can live on milk diets," she told the window. "I can, too." "Third Sorrowful Mystery," she continued around the prescribed circle of beads.

In between prayers, she listened to see if her heartbeat was slowing down. Sometimes its soft thumping unnerved her as she thought of the irregularities that plagued her. If she couldn't find her pulse, she knew her heart had stopped to rest until she could pray again. So many worries filled her mind. She'd asked her daughter, "Why would someone steal the sleeves to my dress patterns? Even though I don't sew anymore, I like to keep them."

Her daughter shrugged and said, "Mama, no one took them. Maybe you lost the patterns or threw them out when you cleaned."

Margaret sighed, "Strange they only took the sleeves. There are people up to no good who sneak in when I'm sleeping. Probably the same people who broke in to use my comb or stole my spoons."

Today, fingers in control, she commanded the beads to resume their travel and murmured, "Fourth Sorrowful Mystery."

Even though she was sweating from the heat, Margaret didn't stop praying to start the fan. Yesterday she couldn't make the button work to make the blades spin. "Maybe it's broken," she sighed, "or maybe I'm the one who's broken."

Margaret concentrated on the most urgent praying of all, the possible kidnapping of her grandchildren. She overheard a cult person talking on TV recently and, in turn, the cult person listened to her conversations inside the trailer. When Margaret told her daughter, the answer was, "You mustn't worry, Mama. Don't think about such things." Then she added, "And please remember to take your meds."

"I don't need pills. I'm not crazy." Margaret was used to her daughter's attitude even toward such important matters. "Kidnapping is serious business." But her words only bounced off her daughter's back.

Her daughter went to the doorway, ready to leave. "Chicken fricassee is in the fridge, Mom. Promise me you'll forget about cults, and remember, the visiting nurse is coming."

Margaret knew the nurse would check her blood pressure and cut her toenails. She filled the plastic dishpan and put her feet to soak as she prayed on. The nurse would ask questions about food and medication. "Best not to mention the poison," Margaret decided. She continued her words of calm. "Blessed is the fruit of thy womb, Jesus." She'd finish the rosary and not think about the problems that plagued her.

"Fifth Sorrowful Mystery. O glorious Queen of all the heavenly host, accept this rosary, which, as a crown of roses, we offer at thy feet."

As the familiar words of the last decade sought the light, Margaret felt her heart loosen its bindings. She closed her eyes and her lips trembled as fragrant rosebuds flew from her mouth, into the warm air, to float gently to the floor. She saw each Hail Mary shaped like a rose, each petal wrapped around a precious word. She inhaled the perfume of flowers that drifted down through the layers of trailer warmth. Magenta petals, like tiny pieces of her heart, fell to the linoleum. Perhaps eventually her heart would disappear, when all the roses stored inside her were gone.

A woman's voice drifted through the screen. "Hello, Margaret, it's the nurse."

Margaret hoped her blood was running through her veins in the right direction. "Just a minute, I'm praying. Now and at the hour of our death, Amen." She crumpled the beads into a ball.

"I'll open the door." She lifted her feet out of the dishpan water and shuffled along the floor, trying to create a path through the petals. She hoped the roses weren't too noticeable. She'd cover her mouth when she spoke, in case more roses appeared even without the prayers. Explaining such things exhausted her.

"On guard, Margaret," she murmured to herself, and opened the door.

"Excuse the mess," she said, "I haven't swept up yet."

Postscript:

Mom prayed until the end of her days at age 94. She was admitted to a general health care facility, and one day I prayed the rosary with her. The next morning I received a call that she'd passed away in the night. I wrote my own words of prayer:

Fragile soul, so close to sleep, so near to dreams,
Enclosed in life's deepening shadows,
The sun shows hot through your thin petals,
Shines and burns through your thin skin,
Cuts through a mind uneasy until prayer transforms to angel song.
Soft, feathered wings reach up in peace.
Soon it will be time to close, a coda from her pale, white lips,
As another frail, old soul escapes toward the sky.

MY HUSBAND DIED TWICE
Marian McCaa Thomas

My husband died twice. I had missed so many of my loved ones' deaths, I wondered if I would miss Tim's, too. In a conversation several months earlier, he had told me, "I don't want to die alone." When he entered the hospital with a broken hip, he was asked if he wanted to sign a Do Not Resuscitate order. He replied, "No! I still have things I want to get done!" So when the aide from the rehabilitation center called me two weeks later to tell me she had found Tim "unresponsive" when she went to check on him, and that he was dead, it was a total shock. She was so blunt! Where was her empathy for me? I had been with Tim for seven hours that day, but had gone home to give Ivy her weekly piano lesson.

That morning, Tim had pleaded, "I really want to go home," and I had replied, "I want you to come home, too, but to do that you have to get stronger, so you have to work hard and do what the physical therapists ask you to do." They came soon after that, and I watched while he put his utmost effort into sitting on the side of the bed, following their instructions to exercise his legs and arms with their help. They lifted him into his wheelchair and he propelled himself to the bathroom, where they lifted him onto the toilet seat. Then he got back into the chair with their help and rolled to the bed. It took 30 minutes of hard work on Tim's part. They congratulated him, and told him he had made good progress. But now I know—he had used his last bit of energy to do the therapy. He was spent. Our daughter Julie came after work, and noticed that he had trouble breathing and ate very little of his dinner. When the aide came to help Tim onto the bedpan, Julie went home, giving her Dad privacy.

Forty minutes after that first phone call, they called again to say that he had been revived. My immediate thought was, "Oh, no! You should have let him die in peace!" I did not want him to suffer yet more indignities. But because he had not signed a DNR document, the rehab staff was required to call paramedics, who came and used CPR to bring Tim back to life—of a sort. Some of his ribs broke under the CPR thrusts, since polio had made them fragile years ago. Because his breathing was so labored, they gave him oxygen and rushed him to the nearest hospital, where he was intubated, just as our beloved son had been in 2020 while dying of leukemia. When I saw him draped in a white sheet, eyes closed, a tube down his throat, my heart went out to him, and I wished his last chapter could have ended differently. But what happened next made me change my mind.

The young medical intern was sympathetic and kind. She and her supervisor explained what was going on, and said they were awaiting the head ER doctor. They offered me water and asked if I would like some time alone with my husband. I said, "Yes." I knew his death was near, but this time, he would not die alone.

I held his warm hand and sang the song which had sustained me sixty years ago, before we were married, when I lived in Korea for a year-and-a-half while he was in grad school in Eugene, Oregon: "Moonbeams," by Victor Herbert. *"Fate may part us, years may pass, future all unknown; still my love shall ever prove faithful to thee, alone."* I had brought Nan C. Merrill's book, *Praying the Psalms*, with me to the emergency room, thinking I might have hours to wait. I read aloud her paraphrase of Psalm 23 about going through the valley of the shadow of death without fear. I sang the Welsh hymn Tim had been singing each morning for the past several weeks: *Guide me, O Thou great Jehovah, pilgrim through this barren land. I am weak, but Thou art mighty, hold me with Thy powerful hand.* Then I simply sat holding his hand, taking in his noble face. When Julie arrived, we sat side-by-side, knowing her father was not long for this world. His breaths were short and shallow, even though aided by machinery.

The hospital chaplain on duty that night was kind and efficient. Giving me papers to sign, she made recommendations about what to do with Tim's body, something I had not thought about at all. She offered a heartfelt prayer. Our son Peter joined us by phone, saying goodbye to his father, assuming, as I had done, that his Dad could hear him although he did not respond. Finally the ER doctor came, and her compassionate expression assured me she felt as I did, that death would be a blessing. After consulting the three of us, she directed the removal of all life support. In the company of his wife and two remaining children, he died quickly and quietly. Not alone.

Julie and I went our separate ways after embracing. There wasn't much sleep that night—maybe a few hours. For those thirty minutes alone with Tim, I will be forever grateful. Perhaps he had sensed that if he signed a DNR, the chances he would die alone were greater than if he didn't. The downhill slide that began with Steven's death at 49 culminated in his own death at 83, just twenty-one months later. They were months marked by his frustration, regret, and diminishing strength, both physically and mentally. To my great relief, they did not last any longer than they did.

Whatever form life takes after death is now known to Tim, and perhaps there is a mystery by means of which he can recognize his son, his parents and grandparents, his dear Aunt Jane, his sister Jennifer, his scientific colleagues who preceded him in death, and a few of the ministers he knew at Linwood Presbyterian Church. If there is a heavenly choir, he is certain to be singing in it!

PAYING TO PEE
Rhonda Wiley-Jones

As a sixty-something woman, I prefer to go in a bathroom rather than the ocean. The necessary jaunt to the closest beach bathroom is plagued with high-season obstacles as I press heel-to-sand-squishing-toes in deep, cool sand. I leave my tangle of friends to fish my way through a knot of tourists; to circumvent an air-born Frisbee flying between two ripped young men; to navigate white lounge chairs and sun-bleached beds; and to duck under and around sunny striped umbrellas.

As I near the eatery that supplies us with a beach *baño*, the aroma of French fries makes my mouth water. Closer still, the smell of grilled pork fills the air with hints of pineapple. I pass the bar with drinking patrons laughing and talking too loud, waiters yelling orders to the kitchen. To the side and back of the restaurant is the bathroom and tip lady. Knowing I don't intend to tip, I avert my eyes from hers.

This newly installed *baño* is built such that the first step is six-inches higher than my stride, the next three are uneven, and there's no handrail. This is the Mexico I know and love. I touch the rough wood of the makeshift structure to steady myself, careful not to splinter a finger. On my way up, a toilet flushes, women speak as if sisters, and spring doors bang shut. The floors are slippery with seawater and sand to my bare feet.

Sure, I use toilet paper, water, soap, and—though they disintegrate—paper towels. I've always been suspicious of paying to pee. Who gets the tips? Is this a way of making money off tourists? I've been in Europe where I had to pay to get into a stall or not go at all.

After washing my hands and slinging them dry, I contemplate my defense—it's inconvenient to carry change when in a swimsuit, nowhere to stow pesos securely and because of that, I'm likely to drop the change in the sand, forever lost.

Today, I offer a nod to the young woman instead of *pesos*. Glancing down at the tip box, I see someone has deposited a twenty-*peso* bill, a dollar at the current exchange rate. I'm not willing to pay a dollar to pee, or anything less.

Several times a day I make the trip, so I slyly observe the local young woman sitting in the scorching sun between the open-air restaurant and the outdoor bathroom. Her thick hair is pulled back off her neck, with a scrunchy holding a fat ponytail. Sans makeup, she endures the sweltering heat.

A notebook lies in her lap with a thick textbook open on the tiny tip table, and pen in hand. As a college academic advisor and instructor, I'm curious. "What are you studying?"

She must understand part of my question because she frowns, thinking, then says something in Spanish, which I don't get, because of my rusty college Spanish.

I try again in English because I don't have the Spanish words. "Textbook? Study?"

She cocks her head sideways, listening for a familiar word.

I try further. "Ah, assignment? Umm, homework?"

"*Sí, sí,* homework." She's pleased she knows the word.

I palm my heart and say in my childlike Spanish, *"Mi nombre es Rhonda."*

She corrects my attempt at an introduction. *"Me llama es Leslie."*

The next day I greet in Spanish, *"Hola, Leslie."*

She lifts her head from her studies to smile and speak. Hoping to generate more conversation, I lean over her open textbook, which appears to be a page of anatomy, and ask, "Nursing homework?"

"Col-lege..." she searches for the next word, "a-na-to-my," then she points in the air to indicate the future. "Homework—to be doctor." Her limited English vocabulary is broader than my Spanish.

"Oh wow! A doctor." She smiles widely, pleased that I get her. After twenty-five years working in higher education, this impresses me—a local Isla Mujeres student preparing for one of the most demanding and honored professions. Island residents have confided to my American and Canadian friends that local schools lack academic rigor. So I hope she is prepared for the road ahead of her. She is doing her part by working hard.

We both try communicating when I stop by, without knowing each other's language. We're successful sometimes.

The skeptic in me says that maybe her book is only high school biology. Maybe she's *not* going to college or even planning to become a doctor. Maybe she's milking a liberal tip from me.

What an unkind thing for me to even think.

Every so often, after the last man leaves the Men's room, Leslie takes her chance to sweep sand from the floor to the front steps and to the sandy beach below. Using an astringent cleaning agent, she wipes down toilets and sinks, which will never look clean regardless of what she does, due to hard seawater. Leslie resupplies toilet tissue and paper towels. She does the same for the Women's room, when the opportunity comes, then places the supplies out of sight and returns to her study table.

Leslie sits with head bent, picks up a pen, places it between her teeth while she opens her text to the same place as before, flipping to the right page. With bowed head, she looks like she might be praying for a way to med school.

I wonder if she receives all or a portion of the tip box. I don't know if she gets a wage for cleaning toilets in addition to tips. She should.

My husband and I spend our days at the beach, then a shower, drinks in our apartment courtyard, and then dinner out, music, and dancing. My daily trip from the beach to our apartment takes me by a coffee hut. Later that week, I see Leslie taking an order behind the counter. She tucks her voluminous hair behind an ear and places a pencil in her mouth while she fills the order.

When she's done, I approach with a smile to say, "Two jobs, Leslie?"

"*Sí*, helping *mi amiga*, the owner."

By creating a connection with Leslie I've come to *want* to help her pay for college and medical school. She's no longer just a face, an entity, another demand for my money as a tourist. She's a young woman with a desire for a future and willingness to work for it. Now I have to admit there is a person with a story behind every tip box or bowl, who works hard and deserves it.

I, too, worked for tips as a waitress during college. I depended on the additional money and remembered the day I got a $5.00 tip for a $6.00 meal. Overcome by that generosity, I ducked my face and headed toward the back of the restaurant to cry with joy.

The memory makes me think twice about paying to pee. Suppressing the skeptic in me, I decide to err on the positive side of Leslie's future—one I wish to support. The following day at the baño, I slip a twenty-peso bill into the tip box. Each time.

LESSONS LEARNED

Lessons on Racism from a Remote Island in Fiji
Kathie Arcide

Paradise is not where you'd expect to uncover your own hidden racism. Here is how it happened.

I was on the vacation-of-a-lifetime with my seven closest friends.

Imagine the bliss of a 95-foot yacht, sailing all around the South Pacific, including the remote Southern Lau Group of islands in Fiji!

We were an amazing group, especially our crew (First Mate, Chef and Deckhand, all from Fiji) and our feisty British Captain, Carol. A nurse, by original profession, Carol is the first female to Captain in the entire Pacific.

We anchored off isolated and beautiful islands, some with tiny villages, but most with no signs of humankind's presence—ever.

These were not your tourist hot spots!

We can all see bigotry in others. It can be blatant, brazen, and rabid, but still easy to deny.

What's happening in the world as I write this, is both heartbreaking and encouraging, none of it a surprise. We hopeful children of the 1950s and '60s believed we were finally beginning to "overcome." We thought we were changing things. But as Reverend Al Sharpton reminded us recently in his eulogy for George Floyd, there is a time and a season for everything, and obviously, we are not there yet.

Recent events have shocked some of us into revisiting our own buried judgments.

I can't describe my dismay at discovering I had undiscovered biases. I was shocked, and so ashamed.

I know I am not alone when I protest proudly, and probably too loudly, that surely *I* am not a bigot, *I* am color blind. But racism is insidious. It is crafty, and sinister, like an undiagnosed deadly disease.

I was raised to be oblivious to racial differences, in a community that, for enough generations, no longer thought twice about these things.

My mother, however, planted a seed in me. She gave up her whole family when she left her childhood religion because of its sanctioned discrimination against Black people.

I thought I was free of racism, growing up in San Diego, immersed in a mixture of ethnicities, from our Latino neighbors and schoolmates to the wide variety of complexions found in any U.S. town with a major Naval Base. As kids, we didn't care about your color nearly as much as what exotic place you came from.

I was a naive adolescent in the racially tumultuous 1960s, and experienced unexpected culture shock moving from the beaches of Southern California to Natchez, Mississippi, whose motto was posted on a giant welcome banner across the main street entrance to town. It boasted: "Where the Old South Still Lives."

There was nothing covert about racism in Natchez back then, with its "Men", "Women" and "Colored" bathrooms, and "Whites Only" public drinking fountains. The town and schools had stayed resolutely segregated, ignoring even Federal mandates.

I was deeply impacted by this experience, a painful awakening that led me directly to Civil Rights work in Alabama just a couple of years later. I was determined, with the passion and grandiose idealism of youth, to end all prejudice.

Well into my forties, I believed that experience of living in the Deep South had surely scrubbed any traces of racism from my psyche.

Back to Paradise:

One spectacular South Pacific day, we hoped to visit an inhabited island. As local custom demanded, we had to get the Village Chief's permission to come ashore. To accomplish this, we sent our 19-year-old Fijian deck hand, Fouro, up a steep hill through thick tropical jungle, to the top of the island where the little village was located.

He returned a couple of hours later, with a cadre of twelve young men, to "escort" us to the village using a shortcut. This required them to slash a path through the jungle. Expecting this, the crew of Fijians came armed with machetes, and other long-bladed knives.

Two of the villagers, along with our three men, set out ahead to make way for our passage up the hill—no small task, believe me! The rest of us hung around on the bright white sandy beach, with water a color there is no word for in the English language. Rocky tide pools filled with beautiful, alien life kept us busy.

There were five women on the shore, and the ten remaining Fijian men.

Suddenly, like lightning striking on a clear, dry day, it happened.

I don't know what triggered it. Maybe it was our guides hovering so closely, waiting to lead us to the village. Maybe it was because they asked so many friendly, but personal questions. Or maybe it was just a glint of sunlight hitting one of the long silver blades they all carried...

But I had a whopper of a PTSD flashback, an instantly incapacitating recall of a horrific event in Alabama 22 years earlier.

I'll spare you the graphic details of the re-activated scene, except to say it involved several men who lured us with *friendly sounding personal questions*, and then offered to *lead us home* safely. Oh, and of course, the fact they had suddenly brandished large silver *knives*.

I had unearthed the trifecta of flashback fodder!

I collapsed on the beach, trembling, terrified, catapulted backwards into that night.

My three women friends, all therapists, guessed before I did what was happening to me, and explained it to our concerned captain. In her capacity as a nurse, she was brilliant in her response.

She sat right down on the sand with me and explained how the people on these remote islands rarely get visitors. Whole generations of natives have never even seen a *Kaivalagi*, (a crazy white person.) She pointed out these "men" I was reacting to, were in fact, just young boys, between eleven and fourteen years old, and were thrilled to guide us safely to and from their village. Their questions provided them an opportunity to gather stories they would share with their village for months to come. They would be Local Heroes!

With captain/nurse Carol's help, I was able to deep-breathe away my panic.

Fijians can be very dark skinned. I did not even consider that I might have also been impacted by their color until much later—either because it was simply not a factor for me, or because I, too, had some deeply hidden racism in me.

Back in that remembered 1968 scene, living as a VISTA Volunteer in a poverty-stricken neighborhood outside Birmingham, Alabama, I hadn't thought much about the fact that those men on that awful night, who "guided us to safety" and later broke into our shack, were Black. I just knew they were men—with knives.

But racism is devious, layered, and without diligent consciousness, it is habitual. One who is truly determined to eradicate it, must be relentless, and can never be too thorough.

Now, all these years later, along with cleaning out my own remaining biases, my ongoing goal is to stop being prejudiced against prejudiced people. I find myself constantly judging bigots. If I hate them for their intolerance, how am I being any different?

I need to find a new way to see things through their eyes—just like Captain Carol showed me in paradise that day.

I never want to forget the power of shifting my perspective from my own damaged history to that of those innocent children, who were thrilled—not scared, curious—not judgmental, fascinated—not repelled.

And who were certainly not a danger to us!

We found out later, during our time in paradise, that in fact, we did have to be cautious and thoughtful around those curious and generous Fijian adolescents—because if we even slightly admired something of theirs, a basket, a mat, a beautiful piece of tapa cloth, even their shoes, they would instantly and enthusiastically insist on giving it to us. Pretty dangerous, eh?

These last two years of pandemic and social unrest, my deepest commitment, passionately fired up once more just like that idealistic teenager I once was, is that when I find myself judging someone for their deep-seated beliefs, I will stop, even if for just a moment. To see through their eyes, I will slip on their lifelong shoes and walk a few steps. I'm not suggesting acceptance or tolerance of harmful behaviors, but I am committed to do the work it will take to find compassion for their story—their *whole* story.

I am committed to not get complacent about my own hidden prejudices, ever again.

REWRITE THE SIGN
Claire Butler

I'd been told countless times that it was a bad thing to give money to the less fortunate who live on the street with their signs. "Buy them a sandwich instead," was the advice. "They will only use the money for drugs or alcohol," was repeated whenever I confessed to making such donations. I'd also heard there were scam artists working the streets in that way—driving away at the end of the day in nice cars. I was torn about not giving money to the homeless because some of them truly were in need; who am I to discern who should receive a hand-up and who should not?

I recently saw a short video, which is now on YouTube, "The Power of Words" by Andrea Gardner, produced by Hay House UK. In it, a man sitting on the sidewalk of a busy street had a sign that read, "I'm blind, please help." He had his cup on the walk in front of him. He was receiving very little attention and not much in the way of support. A woman passing by stopped, turned his cardboard sign over and rewrote his sign. The man could tell she was writing on his sign; he bent forward to feel her shoes, clearly perplexed. She walked away without saying a word to him.

Within a few minutes money was pouring into his cup. At the end of the day, the same woman stopped in front of him. He recognized her footfalls and again felt her shoes. "What did you do to my sign?" he asked her. "I wrote the same thing but in a different way." The camera panned down to the new sign: "It's a beautiful day and I can't see it." At that moment I recognized empathy. People empathized with the man because he could not see the beautiful day. It was something they could relate to. The reality of not being able to see a beautiful day had opened their minds to the powerful loss that man had suffered—they empathized.

It suddenly became clear to me why I had felt so strongly about giving to people on the street when I encounter them: there but for the grace of God go I. We have no promises of health, safety, food, or shelter. In one second, our lives could change by some disaster, sending any one of us into poverty with an inability to work.

My outlook was changed by that video, and the word empathy became a breathing entity for me. I no longer struggle with giving to those who are on the street, doing what they need to do to survive. It's not my concern what they do with the money I give them—the signs in my head and on my heart have been rewritten to give without compunction.

Field of Dreams
Sara Etgen-Baker

We stood outside the dilapidated picket fence and shaded our eyes, casting our gazes across the grassy pasture of old man Buhler's farmland. His thriving cotton farm had once been one of the largest in the region—more than twenty acres of land near the center of town. When hard times prevailed, old man Buhler sold all but a few acres of his farm to a developer, who converted the acreage in 1951 to suburban city streets with row upon row of small tract houses. Smack dab in the middle of this development was what remained of the Buhler property—a two-acre field with a farmhouse, where old man Buhler lived alone and tended his sheep.

I lived directly across the street from that field, its weeds and tall grasses surrounding the tired and weary farmhouse. The house wore the color of unfinished wood, weathered for countless years by harsh elements and baked by the hot summer sun. Like old man Buhler himself, it faced our neighborhood proudly, almost defiantly, with its rusted tin roof and sagging porch. In the summer, the smells of dried grass and sun-warmed earth from Buhler's field were like a siren's song compelling my friends and me to ignore his *NO TRESPASSING* sign, climb over his fence, and explore the vast region that lay before us.

Our explorations were harmless curiosity until the fateful day we decided to transform part of Buhler's field into a baseball diamond—our very own field of dreams. We commandeered a portion of his field and spent days trampling over the tall, dry, inflexible grass until it was flattened—making sure, though, to keep the surrounding grass intact so as to camouflage and shield ourselves from old man Buhler's scrutinizing eyes.

Afterward, we began our mornings by hauling our equipment across the street and tossing it over the old man's fence. And we most certainly had no sophisticated or costly baseball equipment—just a rather large, thick stick; one tattered baseball; an assortment of well-worn baseball gloves; and three metal trash can lids that served as bases. Once over the fence, we each took our designated positions on the makeshift diamond, spending our summer days whiling away the hours playing baseball in old man Buhler's field with him being none the wiser.

That is, until the day we happened upon a discarded, cracked baseball bat lying alongside the curb in front of my house. We filled the crack with rubber cement, wrapped it in duct tape, and headed over to Buhler's field where, one at a time, we each practiced swinging the bat at a pitch. We weren't used to the weight and feel of a *real* bat, so we mostly just hit grounders and pop-ups somewhere in the infield. Three of us eventually made it to base; that's when my brother, Eddie, came up to bat.

He planted his feet firmly and tapped the bat on the ground, signaling the pitcher that he was ready. First, the windup then the pitch—a fastball fired straight toward the catcher and across home plate. Eddie swung and leaned into the pitch; the bat struck the ball. Crack! The bat splintered into a gazillion pieces at Eddie's feet. "It's going….going….Gone!" We went wild, and those of us on base rounded our way around the bases screaming and shouting. "It's a homerun! It's a homerun!"

But then we heard glass shattering and knew the ball had flown through a glass window at the farmhouse. Almost immediately, old man Buhler bolted out of his house and barreled his way across his property shouting, "Get out of here you good-for-nothing kids! Ain't 'cha got no respect? Can't 'cha read the 'NO TRESPASSING' sign?!"

We grabbed our gear and hightailed it over the fence with Buhler hot on our heels. We ran at white-hot speed into my backyard, seeking refuge underneath Dad's upturned flat-bottom boat. Hunkered down in the shadows, we hid, quaking and sweating, and held our breaths, silently waiting as old man Buhler approached the boat, stopping just inches from our faces.

Looking out from the darkness, I saw his brown leather boots, their leather creased and weathered, their laces frayed, and their soles worn through. Seconds later, Mother emerged from her kitchen into the backyard.

"What are you doing in my backyard?" Mother asked him.

"I'm looking for those dang kids!" he said in an explosive voice.

"What kids? What on earth for?"

"They busted out a window in my house. Windows are expensive, ya know. Someone's gotta pay!"

Mother reached inside her apron pocket, retrieved a $20 bill, and handed it to him. "Will this cover the damage?"

Buhler snatched the $20 from Mother's hand, mumbled, and retreated in the direction of his field.

After Mother went inside, we kids scrambled out from under the boat.

"Do you think we got away with it?" Eddie asked me.

"I doubt it. We'll probably be grounded."

Days passed, and Mother said nothing to us about the broken window and the $20 she forked over to Mr. Buhler. Perhaps Eddie was right. Maybe Mother didn't know we were the kids who'd broken old man Buhler's window. But guilt sat heavy inside my heart, and I eventually confessed.

"I apologize, Mother, for Mr. Buhler's broken window."

"I'm not the one you need to apologize to. You must apologize to Mr. Buhler."

"Go over there all by myself?"

"Yes, ma'am. The sooner the better. He deserves your respect."

I remember that day with great clarity. I walked over to Buhler's property, trudged across the field to his barn, and hesitated before walking inside. The barn, filled with old-timey farming implements and tools, was like traveling back in time when cotton was king in Texas. Along one wall, he'd thumbtacked pictures that told the tale of his younger days, tending his cotton field with his wife, children, and farm hands. One picture in particular grabbed my attention. Mr. Buhler was standing with his wife in the middle of his vast cotton field with truckloads of recently harvested cotton behind him, his face beaming with pride.

"What cha' doing in here, kid?" Mr. Buhler's raspy voice startled me.

I turned in his direction and immediately noticed how different his face was now; it was sad, leathery looking, and creased like his shoes, evidence of his rugged life and resilient character.

I put myself in his worn-out shoes and suddenly understood why he was cranky and angry with us. He was old and alone, his wife of many years having long-since passed. Something inside me shifted, and I realized that the little patch of land on which his farm now sat was all that remained of that bygone time and the dreams of a younger, more vibrant man. This was Buhler's field of dreams, not ours, and we kids *had been* disrespectful.

"Mr. Buhler," I said my voice cracking. "I apologize for coming onto your property. I had no right to do so. Please forgive me for being disrespectful. It'll never happen again."

To my surprise, he said nothing. He just lifted a single eyebrow and stared at me in disbelief. He cleared his throat to speak. But before he could, I turned tail and ran home, never looking back and never again venturing onto Buhler's property, having learned an invaluable lesson: respect for another human being comes from willingly putting myself in another person's shoes and experiencing life from his perspective. I later learned that quality is empathy, the capacity to compassionately inhabit the consciousness of another human being.

As I matured into womanhood, empathy allowed me to better relate to my spouse, stepchildren, family, friends, co-workers, and even strangers, resulting in healthier relationships. On a larger scale, empathy created tolerance in me for others who were different from myself, and it dissipated the likelihood of angry, unresolved disputes.

From a global perspective, empathy is infinitely important, especially because it leads to compassion—the type of compassion that pushes people to dive in and help people they don't know or people they've never met, particularly when a major disaster occurs. Empathy is what makes us wonderfully human. Without it, the world would be a less humane and less functional place in which to live.

Will Work For Food
Linda Healy

Taking longer at the grocery store than anticipated, I was rushing to pick up my daughter from school. This was a day in 1992 when I would learn a lot about empathy.

While we were at a red light, my 7-year-old son, Matthew, said, "Mommy, why are those people sitting over there and what does the sign say?" Looking to the right I saw a man, a woman, and a toddler sitting by an abandoned building, holding a sign that said, "Will work for food." Their clothes were torn, and they were sitting on a dirty blanket. I saw a duffel bag, a diaper bag, an umbrella stroller, and an almost empty bag of disposable diapers, as well as a nearly empty jug of red Kool-Aid. The child was sitting in her mother's lap. She had dirt and food on her face, matted blond hair, big blue eyes, and a beautiful smile. The mother had on shorts, and I could see her legs were sunburned and looked painful. As soon as my eyes focused on this couple and their little girl, a huge lump came up in my throat and tears came to my eyes.

The light changed and I began to drive on to school to pick up my daughter. I could hardly see as tears poured down my cheeks. I could not answer Matthew's questions for some time. I felt sensitive to the plight of this family. How do you explain to your sheltered child that some people don't have a place to live or food to eat?

This time I could not appease my conscience by simply going back and giving them money, as I had done with people I had seen on the streets before. They needed real help with their problems. It seemed right to help them; no other option entered my mind.

After I picked up my daughter, I drove back to them. The man ran to my car, introduced himself. "I'm George, and this is my wife, Tiffany. This here is our little girl, Amber." Then he asked, "Do you have any work for me?"

I said, "I do not, but how can I help?"

Without any hesitation, George said, "Diapers." I asked if they had food and he said, "A couple of sandwiches." George went on, "I worked in the oilfields but there has been no work recently. Because of the type of job I had, I couldn't collect unemployment, so we lost our home. Some weeks earlier we sold the car for food and rent money."

I asked, "Where are you staying?"

He replied, "A weekly hotel but the rent was due at 12 noon. We had no money, so we had to get out."

I promised, "I will return with diapers."

At the grocery store, it seemed I could not stop things from jumping into the basket: bread, peanut butter, spam, diapers, wipes, apples, oranges, bananas. When I returned to George and Tiffany, it was 5 p.m. on Friday, so I took them back to the motel where they had been staying and paid for another week. I believed this would give me some time to help them find more assistance.

On the way to the motel, I asked where they thought they might have stayed that night. George said, "We didn't know. We were scared. We were just sitting there praying for something to happen. And it did! You came." Again, tears sprang to my eyes. Could I really be the answer to someone's prayers?

The motel was rundown. The room smelled of mold. The bedspread was faded, as was the only chair in the room. George and Tiffany were jubilant. You would have thought I had taken them to a palace. They asked, "How can we repay you?"

I suggested, "Someday help someone else." George and Tiffany agreed that they would. George's face relaxed and for the first time I saw him smile.

George told me that a man had stopped while I was gone to the grocery and offered George $35 to clean his yard the next day. George seemed very glad. I gave them my phone number and I took the number at the motel.

The next week my call to the welfare system was less than satisfying. I was told that I shouldn't pick up strangers; they might hurt or rob me.

I should have enough to keep me busy at home with my job and my children.

I was asked if I was rich enough to help every homeless person I passed? If so, they would be glad to put me on their list of resources.

There was a system to help these people. I should know that and so should "they."

Hadn't I seen this family on the street before?

They were beggars and didn't really want to work.

I couldn't even argue. I felt sorry for this worker's apparent burnout. My experience with George and Tiffany told me a different story. Never for one moment did it cross my mind that George did not want to work. The only words I had left to say were not kind, so I said goodbye to the welfare system.

George called me a few days later and said he was offered a construction company job in Houston, 300 miles away, and asked me for money to get to there.

I told George it was a very busy week in our area (the rodeo and carnival were in town). I said he might work a couple of days to earn the money. My hope was George would feel empowered and independent if he could do this on his own.

George was concerned that he might lose the job if he did not go immediately to Houston. He asked me to call the construction company and vouch for him and see if they would hold the job a few days for him. I did so, and yes, there really was a job! They would hold it for him.

George and Tiffany made it to Houston and started a new life. And I helped a little. I cherished knowing them and will never forget them.

I learned there was no need to judge why someone needed help, just help. I hope my children learned that from me. It was a huge lesson in empathy for us and some of the best money I ever spent!

Communal Ties
Shawn Marie LaTorre

Empathy and humor share a connection. Empathy begins when we learn to be better people, understanding that our lives are closely linked to the lives of others. Humor can serve as a vehicle for that.

Laughter has been said to be the best medicine, and I'm of the opinion, being the oldest girl in a family of nine, that we shared far too little of it for all the duties our lives entailed growing up! I do, however, remember watching a late night television show with my dad called *Candid Camera*, directed by Allen Funt. The two of us would laugh so hard I kept a hanky nearby to wipe the tears from my eyes whenever we watched it. My father, a practical joker himself, found this hidden camera set up for unsuspecting people completely up his alley! The hidden camera, always revealed to the "victims" at the end, rendered the jokes harmless and left everybody laughing.

Then there was my summer stint with a tape recorder. I've been both a radio host and a radio talk show guest, many times actually. It all started with the creation of my own call-in radio show. I captured each radio program on a small black tape recorder that I kept in a tiny closet of my room. The voices for both the interviewer and all the call-in guests for the program were mine! I was maybe ten or eleven at the time. Sitting next to the big black two-part telephone, I'd record the sound of the receiver ringing, being picked up, and then set back down at the end of each call. (I figured out how to make our phone ring by dialing our own number and quickly hanging up.)

My radio program's purpose was to focus on problems within the community that weren't getting as much attention as citizens thought they should. One frequent female caller complained about people stepping on bugs—ladybugs, usually. Clearly the little darlings could be seen trying to get to the other side of the sidewalk. People just needed to watch where they were going! Another ranted about people spitting in public places, open lots, or even grassy areas where barefoot children might scamper during the summer months. Couldn't people understand that germs enter homes in the most unexpected of ways? One of the more unmistakable voices was that of a raspy, ornery old man with a very deep voice. He was a frequent caller, whose voice was hard for me to maintain for long, so he usually ranted wildly on some topic such as people burping in public, or casting their shopping carts in the general direction of the cart corral (in the parking lot of our neighborhood Thrifty Acres) only to nick a nearby vehicle in the process. He'd go on for just a minute about how and where he'd seen such behavior, insist people were complete idiots, and promptly hang up.

Oh, what I wouldn't give to have the tape recordings of any one of those radio shows. I can still see my mother throwing her head back and laughing so hard she'd cry at my semi-professional presentations of community concerns from a juvenile perspective. I varied the voices and complaints when I was in this recording phase, but the general topic of outrage never changed. Perhaps this was an early indicator of my interest in social justice.

Some of the things we kids found humorous, our parents did not. For example, the plastic bags that Mom put in her boots each winter. We laughed and begged her to roll the tops of those Wonder Bread bags with the brightly colored polka dots down so folks wouldn't see them. She saw no reason to act like an RB (rich bugger), she'd say, throwing on an old, shabby jacket just for effect. I wondered if I should tell her or my dad that I didn't think we were the best candidates to be living in this part of town? No, that would crush their very hardworking spirits. We were on the rise, my dad was sure of it.

There was a time Mom swung a large stick at a bat that got into the house, perhaps coming up from the cellar. She missed the bat, but seriously injured our ancient cat, who died the next day. Who knew Fluff had finally dragged himself off the register where he warmed himself and was standing so close to watch the action? Some of my brothers found this amusing, but I was crushed at losing this feeble feline, who'd wandered onto our stoop so many winters ago. Seeing my tears, my brothers surrounded me with hugs and promises that we'd get a new one soon.

Then there was the time my two brothers and I, seated in the back of my father's rusty Buick, started guffawing, snorting, and groaning about a nearby car spewing so much exhaust we could hardly breathe, even with the windows up. We asked my dad to pull up alongside at the stoplight, so we could hold our noses to let the male driver know that we thought his car stunk. Well, the quick hand of justice flew back, hitting my oldest brother Charlie smack on the top of his head. That shut us all up. We got a quick lesson in empathy that morning. We hadn't considered that this man perhaps didn't want to drive a car like that, but maybe didn't have other means. We'd initially thought this was funny. My dad failed to see the humor, and shared his wisdom with us as this opportunity presented itself. We drove the rest of the way downtown to his pharmacy feeling ashamed of ourselves.

Seems like people who struggle love to pinpoint someone more miserable than they are just to make themselves feel better situated in life. Now that we kids have grown up to be somewhat "better situated," we haven't forgotten lessons learned nor the value of empathy in bringing a community together.

Soaking Up Early Lessons on Ecology
Melanie McGauran

I was ten years old when I first saw the December 1970 cover of *National Geographic* magazine. Folded around bills and placed neatly in the letterbox by our front door, I pulled it out when I got home from school. I didn't realize it then, but it was a pivotal moment when I separated the mail from the magazine and glanced at its cover.

The photograph was a close-up of a bird, which I later learned was a western grebe. She was swimming off a beach, but oil covered every feather. She looked slick and black. There had been an oil spill off the coast of California in 1969 and National Geographic wanted to research the growing crisis of how our human population was damaging the environment and the plants and creatures who also live in it.

I could not stop looking at the bird. I tried to imagine what she was thinking. Was she panicked, feeling this unknown and unwelcome weight on her? Did she have that innate instinct that she was dying? I wondered how long she could survive. An hour? A day? I was looking at a death sentence on the cover of a magazine. I hated that reality, but embraced the message. It was vital to protect our world's ecology.

It was barely a year later when the same theme emerged again. In 1971, the Keep America Beautiful organization started an iconic anti-littering campaign. The public service announcement depicted a Native American man shedding a tear at the sight of trash landing at his feet by the side of the road. The slogan was, "People start pollution. People can stop it." This time, the message came right through the close-up of the man's eyes. He may have been an actor, but he was representing a group of people whose way of life always respected the land that we were busy trashing.

I absorbed his tear, instantly becoming cognizant of every paper scrap, cup, or bag I used in public and I always found a trashcan. I never littered out of a car window and grew frustrated at the number of drivers who did.

This isn't a story about a girl who grew up, destined to join National Geographic or The Nature Conservancy, but it is about one girl who internalized what she saw and vowed to protect the planet.

As I grew older, I helped pick up trash around our local lakes. I stopped using straws and store bags when I was only purchasing a couple of items. I was lucky to live in an area that supported a recycling program. As the PTA volunteer once responsible for hiring talent for school assemblies, I hired a musical group on Earth Day that used songs and visuals to help the students open themselves to our environment. I do not know whether the concept stayed or affected future behavior, but I understood it was worth trying.

Since the day I pulled the mail from the letterbox so many years ago, pollution has gotten more complicated, with products like plastic microbeads—used in hundreds of beauty creams and lotions—which slip by filters and end up in rivers and seas, killing marine wildlife. There are floating masses of plastic trash now in our oceans. The largest one contains 79,000 tons of plastic. It lies in the Pacific, between Hawaii and California.

Fortunately, there is an almost-equal opposite force for conservation in play. Through recycling efforts, experts are turning trash into usable goods, such as sleeping bags, lawn furniture, and greeting cards. I read that about 35% of trash is now recyclable. Preventing certain products or packaging from even being introduced to the consumer market is another big step towards cleaning up our world.

I thought about the western grebe last year when the opportunity arose to protect a bird, which had built a nest on the edge of my front garden. She was a Common Nighthawk, a species of bird that builds its nests on the ground. Her camouflaged coloring was excellent, but I spotted movement one day as she shifted her body around her eggs.

I started to watch her daily from the window, sometimes facing high winds and driving rain, never once budging from her eggs. When the landscapers arrived, I blocked off her nest and told them to stay away. This went on for several weeks until I noticed a baby head beneath her.

"Oh!" I exclaimed when I realized there were two.

A single photo of a bird's plight sparked a lifelong promise to contribute to a healthier ecology. My contributions may be smaller moments, but I have practiced them for a lifetime. I am also confident that I am not alone, and when combined with the promises from thousands of others who felt that same message, I like to think that we have made an impact.

The Gifts of Fiction
Margaret Dubay Mikus

Inspired by "Discovery of Witches" TV series, based on books by Deborah Harkness.

Once again
I am in love with
a fictional character
brought to life
by a skilled actor
infused with humanity
by the original author
adapted by a brave screenwriter
who like gods
created the world
and filled it with
all manner of creatures
who looked real
even in imagination
and sounded real
and moved to tears
or joy, the shadows and
the light streaming
Time not being linear
drawing us in
always desiring more
not wanting the story to end
compelling us to see, feel
understand, comprehend, reveal
heal, even temporarily
something of ourselves.

LESSON LEARNED IN A BATHROOM STALL
Erin Philbin

It is June, 1980. I've just turned 19, and I'm preparing for my first undergraduate clinical practicum as a speech language pathologist. I'm shy by nature and am not quite certain how I chose a career where I would be providing therapy to people I don't even know. I'm even more afraid of telling my mother that I may want to change my major. Before I know it, I'm scheduled to see my first patient.

When our clients are assigned, I assume that they will be young children working on their speech sounds during their summer break. One by one, my friends are provided with charts of kids with completed evaluations, goals, progress notes and activities from previous summer sessions. I am the last to be provided with a therapy folder. It is suspiciously thin. A short note is taped to the front directing me to meet with the director of the program after I have reviewed the sparse information provided.

My initial doubts have turned to abject fear. My very first client is to be a young woman a few years older than I, who has sustained a head injury from a car accident. I know nothing about head injuries. I have not had a class that addressed language and cognitive issues in adults. I am terrified. The director of the program tells me that she will be my advisor for the semester as she begins to gather reading material for me from her private library.

While my friends plan cute activities for their clients and shop for scratch-and-sniff stickers as rewards, I am buried in textbooks and journal articles about brain injury. I have no idea how I am going to help a young woman who has had her entire life change in an instant.

The day of the first therapy session I am so nervous, I am certain I am going to be sick. I cannot stay out of the restroom. It is almost time for the session to begin when I hear the lavatory door open, and two women enter. An older voice says, "You're going to be late. You've been procrastinating all morning."

A scared voice answers, "I don't think I want to do this today. I don't even know this woman!" The realization hits me that this is my client! She is just as scared as I. My focus immediately changes. Although I am still terrified, I want to help her feel less anxious. My attention turns to how I can help her relax. The girl and her mom take a few moments to collect themselves before leaving the bathroom. I slip out after them and a few moments later, introduce myself and begin my first therapy session.

For the past 42 years, I have dedicated my career to working with adults, focusing on those with head injuries. I have worked with more patients than I can count; yet deep down I am still that shy person. Every time I start with a new patient, I am reminded of that young woman and draw some courage for the person in front of me. I meet their eyes with a smile and say, "Hi. I'm Erin, your speech therapist. Let's see what we can do to make things a little easier for you today."

Empathy is Emotional Mindfulness
Sandra Stanko

Empathy is emotional mindfulness, which

Means seeing the whole

Person and being

Attentive to

The feelings, experiences, dreams, and sufferings

However

You are able.

KJ The Empathetic Cat
Marian McCaa Thomas

I didn't want KJ at first. My daughter found her trying to cross a busy street, rescued her and brought her home. My first word upon seeing the tiny black and white kitten was, "NO!" I love birds, and I thought of cats as bird-killers. But my "NO!" was no match for my daughter's love for KJ. Since my husband was allergic to animal danders, KJ had to be an "outside cat," so we built her a small wooden house and placed it on the front porch facing south so in the winter the sun would warm her a bit. In the years she lived with us, if she did kill any birds or mice, she didn't bring them to her cat house, and I never found any dead birds or mice in our yard.

During the first few years we had KJ, our daughter had the usual teen angst, plus extra identity issues because she was adopted. She had two older brothers who were excellent students, and she was always being compared to them. To her, school wasn't as important as having friends. When things got tense in our house, I would sometimes go out on the porch and sit on the swing that hung from the porch ceiling. That's when KJ would jump up on the swing and settle herself in my lap, purring contentedly and letting me stroke her fur, which was as soft as a rabbit's coat. Her purring and calm demeanor always helped me breathe more slowly and deeply. I sensed that she understood how badly I needed to calm down.

She was companionable in another way: our house had a detached garage, and there were five steps up to a landing and another five steps up to the porch, which wrapped around the front and side of the house. When my car pulled into the driveway, KJ would run out to meet me and stay beside me as I hurried up those steps and across the porch to the front door. But when my husband came home, it was an entirely different story. He wore leg braces and walked with crutches, having contracted polio as a teenager. After running out to meet him, KJ stayed right beside him as he got out of his car. He walked carefully and slowly, so she walked beside him slowly. When he got to the steps, he grasped the railing with his hand, pulled one leg up to the next step, and then grasped the rail further up and pulled his other leg up onto that same step. It was a slow process, which was repeated for each step. She stayed right beside him, matching his slow pace the way she had matched my speed—the companion we each needed.

I learned from KJ's example to be more patient with my husband's slow pace, accepting him fully just the way he was, adjusting to his needs as they kept changing. KJ lived only sixteen years, but it was long enough to teach me to be more empathetic to people of differing abilities. Service dogs are trained to help humans with physical or emotional needs, and I'm convinced cats could be used in the same capacity, if they were all like KJ the empathetic cat!

GIVING AND RECEIVING

Five Women Around a Table
Sharon L. Charde

Theresa, replete with tattoos and a large silver cross that nestled between her generous breasts, settled in next to me in one of the hard gray plastic chairs circling the big table in the shelter's common room. When I realized I'd forgotten to bring up the notebooks and pens I'd brought for the group, she quickly volunteered to go down to my car and get them.

I must have looked quizzical.

"You can trust me," she said, with a large smile. "I've been here for nine months. I'm not going anywhere. I don't even remember how to drive." The others chorused their agreement. So, I gave this woman I'd just met, who later told me she'd been strung out on crack for 31 years and did everything and anything she could to feed her habit, the keys to my red Saab.

We sat around a long rectangular table much too big for our small group. A strikingly beautiful Latina, hair pulled back in a neat bun, planted herself far down on the side opposite from me. I asked her to move in closer—I couldn't hear her when she spoke—and her face scrunched in worry.

"I don't trust people enough to be that close," she said.

But she hesitantly moved nearer to Fatima, who sat directly across from me. Fatima's face and skin were flecked with red dots of what appeared to be insect bites, or maybe adolescent pimples, though she'd told me she was 32. She desperately wanted the book I'd brought, *Success Looks Good on Me*. I'd specially ordered it at the request of a woman who'd been at the last group meeting. She wasn't here, and no one even remembered her until I offered a description.

"Oh, she left a while ago," said Dania, the queenly African American woman who was the city shelter's program manager and had organized this group. "We found a placement for her."

Handing Fatima the book, along with a copy of *I Am Not a Juvenile Delinquent*, the anthology of poems written by my at-risk girls, which I'd brought for everyone, I quietly sighed.

She grabbed one quickly, saying she'd already read it and marked many of the poems for her adolescent daughter.

"Oh, did you get it from one of the other residents here?" I asked. I'd brought copies the last time I'd come.

"No, it was on a shelf with some other books at CVH and I read it there. I am so happy to have my own copy!" The women and girls mouthed acronyms constantly. They were almost always for programs or places new to me; but I did know Connecticut Valley Hospital and wondered, with pleasure, how my collection of the Touchstone girls' poems had gotten there.

I'd brought another "Twelve Steps for Women" workbook and she wanted that, too.

"Well, maybe you can share," I said, looking worriedly at the other women who were not as aggressive in claiming any of the stuff I'd brought. "I gave the other ones away last time I was here."

Nobody responded.

Next to me on the other side was an African American woman so slim and dark and quiet that she seemed shadow-like. "This is the one I'll have to work hard at drawing out," I thought. I was to be right about that.

"I have an anger problem," she said repeatedly. "So I keep to myself."

Theresa returned with my car keys, the notebooks, and another 12-step workbook I'd not realized I had. I was relieved, now that each could have her own copy. "I've already worked the steps," she said, "but you can never do it too many times."

"Do all of you have substance abuse problems?" I asked.

"Yup," Theresa answered for everyone. "I'm clean two years now." Fatima was five months, the Latina woman nine months, the shadowy woman wouldn't say. "I keep to myself," she repeated.

They each clamored to tell their wrenching stories. They'd lost their children, their homes, their husbands, their cars, and their bank accounts. Crack and heroin had wrested their lives from their former worlds into this one, a supported living shelter in Hartford's inner city. Tears fell so hard that Theresa went off to get paper towels from the bathroom, since I'd forgotten tissues and there weren't any in the large grim room in which we were meeting.

I spoke, too, telling them of my son's death and how it had brought me to writing, how writing could be healing, how I'd found the Touchstone girls and worked with them for fifteen years, knowing the world needed to hear their stories.

"And yours, too," I said, looking out at their tearful faces. "The world needs to know what brought you here. It's so willing to write you off, write off the girls, ignore you as losers, say why don't they just get a job, shape up."

"I can't imagine losing a child," Theresa said, reaching out for my hand. "It's the worst thing that could ever happen to anyone."

They all repeated the words I'd heard so many times, shaking their heads in horror at the thought of losing their own children, these women who seemed to have already lost everything. But it was true, their children, though not with them, *were* still alive. And they were struggling with what it would take to get their lives back, piece by piece, to let go of the siren call of the drugs that they still craved.

"You lose who you are," the Latina woman declared in her soft voice, wiping her tears with the paper towel Theresa had brought her. "You're just nothing. The drug takes you. You don't care what you do to get it. You're no one."

"How did your son die?" Fatima wanted to know. So, I told the story again, the wall, Rome, the asthma, the branch in his hand, the worry about foul play. The poems about all of it. They wanted me to read my poems, and listen to the radio broadcast the BBC had commissioned.

"But we have to stop talking and write," I said. "The minutes are ticking away, and we only have until 2:45." I gave them prompts from the poems of a former Touchstone girl, whose work I'd just copied to send her. She was in her twenties now, I told them, she's got a child, a job, has taken some college courses and will be married in October. And her mother was in jail for drugs her whole life. She's making it.

I wanted them to hear the success, that it was possible.

I read Marissa's poems to them. "The Hardest Thing I've Ever Done," "Secrets," "If I Could, I Would."

They wrote their words eagerly, quickly, all but the shadowy woman next to me. "I don't write well," she murmured. "I keep to myself. I have an anger problem."

"Write about that," I said. "Just write about anything. You can do it." And slowly, she did. She read with all of us, hesitantly at first, and then came out of the shadows to really join in.

No one wanted the group to end. I didn't either. We all embraced and told each other how much we looked forward to our next meeting.

Why do I only feel whole and human with these women, these girls, the world says are broken? Why do I only here feel like myself, in a way I never do any other time?

These women, who have lost everything, who have done what the world calls unspeakable—prostituting, stealing, doing drugs, abusing their children, having them taken away—they are fully human.

I'm not.

I always want to wrap things up neat and nice, finish them, and move on to the next task on my list. I'm impatient, compulsive, prone to painful relationships with remote un-giving people that mirror mine with my mother, that leave me starving and lost. I'm judgmental and intense, a perfectionist.

But when I'm with these women and girls, the homeless, the shattered, I'm not any of those things. I lose myself in their presence; I become real, like they are.

I become the self I want to be.

We are all so human together.

MAKE IT MATTER THAT IT DID
Christine Hassing

I didn't recognize him at first. I thought we were strangers. Until the first moments we met became several minutes later.

Until he softly spoke *no thank you*. The only one respectfully declining the blank piece of paper I was handing him.

Of course, recognition doesn't always come immediately. At least not on the surface. Somewhere deep within me stirred awake though, opening my ears. And my heart.

Three words he spoke. Only three. It only took three to hear a story he wasn't speaking.

I continued standing in front of each of the others in the room, one by one. Each eagerly taking the blank piece of paper, anticipating what they could write or draw to share what hope meant to them.

I heard whispers as the teacher leaned close to him, gently inquiring, and then encouraging him to reconsider.

Then his next five words felt like a poke inside me, like a finger jab just to make sure I hadn't fallen back asleep.

It won't be good enough.

The teacher assured him that whatever he drew or wrote would be. He quietly got up from his seat, walked over to where I sat, and asked for a piece of paper.

He was the first to finish his drawing. He wanted me to see it. But not others. Because.

Nobody likes me, he whispered, when I exclaimed what a great drawing it was and asked if I could keep it.

His head nod gave approval. His smile lifted his shoulders, a hesitant taller stance communicating gladness to be seen by a stranger.

Positively.

Or perhaps to be seen. Period.

I thought we were strangers. Until the first moments we met became several days later. And I could not stop thinking of him.

I was wide-awake.

And then I remembered the leadership philosophy I had written when finishing my M.A. in Organizational Leadership. Because of.

Because of.

Because I once was seeking hope and faith in the painful ebbs of life, I hold compassion for those who seek purpose in what they currently cannot explain. Because I have experienced self-worthlessness, I empathize with others who are searching for self-worth.

Because I know the feeling that my voice is not worthy of being heard, I can hear the voices of others that are not able to find their own voice to speak.

And then I fully recognized him!

He is.

Who I was at his age.

I wore visible labels such as "quiet," "shy," "smart," "good girl," and "sweet." Inside, I was framing my story with the titles "Not Enough," "Be Seen, Not Heard," "On Second Thought, Don't Be Seen," and "Maybe Striving for Perfection Will Equal Achieving Feeling Worthy."

I pondered what labels he was wearing.

I remembered a study a military veteran verbally shared with me when I was writing my second book. He didn't name the study, but shared how it had evaluated active duty and retired military who experienced the more significant elements of P.T.S.D. (Post Traumatic Stress Disorder). What was learned is that one of two experiences had happened for these individuals.

Either an individual had experienced a "perfect" childhood into and through high school that included happily married parents, most popular student, captain of sports teams, valedictorian, and so forth.

When these individuals with "perfect" lives experienced trauma, it turned life upside down for them, so to speak.

Or an individual had experienced trauma as a child and did not have a way of reframing their story, so when they experienced significant trauma again as an adult, it only intensified the experience, opening the past wounds of unresolved emotional pain and scars.

Reframed stories.

What if children could be given an opportunity to write their life stories thus far? What if a child could have the opportunity to frame—or reframe—their story to ensure it was filled with gratitude and love? With worthiness? With purpose and resilience, if the story already contains a painful paragraph or chapter?

About thirty years ago, a friend reframed a story for me. I had heard a news story of a tragic car accident, and though I didn't know the father and two children who did not survive, nor the mom and newborn baby who had stayed home and not made the travels, I could not shake that story from my thoughts. In seeing my struggle, my friend shared words of wisdom with me that became a seed he planted, I watered, and it continues to branch out from my heart, informing how I see and hear life's moments. It continues to greatly influence my teaching, coaching, and writing.

Christine, everything that happens—good, as well as tragic—is planned. If you make a positive change in your life because of this accident—perhaps you drive slower when the roads are icy, or you express love more frequently—you will give purpose to why this accident happened. You will make it matter that it did. My friend from that time doesn't know that from his brief message with this gifted seed, I would build a solid root system around this mantra.

Nothing is coincidence; there is purpose in everything that takes place. Life does not shelter us from challenge or loss, but we can make it matter when it occurs. Life's downturns are the gifts to help us grow.

My friend paused to listen for the words I wasn't saying, then he graciously listened to the words I spoke and handed me a reframed story I could refer to for life.

So back to the teacher I went now, with a seed of my own to hand to her. Her students could write their life stories. I would act as "writing coach" through the development of their completed stories.

The teacher gave homework assignments that included the stories of their birth, the members of their family, a favorite aspect of each of their family members, a favorite memory, and what an adult family member remembered about being their age in school. Through each of the one-on-one sessions, I would have the privilege of hearing stories filled with a beautiful blend of innocence and wisdom, happiness and love, gratitude, and imagination.

He didn't have all the pieces of his story. He only had one element. A favorite memory. That, when listened to, was a favorite wish because the memory was unpleasant.

In that way that life magically connects moments before we know they will connect, I had his picture from a few weeks before. The one that represented what hope was to him. The one that would fuel my imagination to create a reframed story, so that when each of the students were handed their few pages of a typed life story in framed binders, he would receive a binder with several pages to his story, too.

A framed—and reframed—story of worth. And happiness. And possibility.

I don't know what he might do with his written story as his life story continues. I hold hope and intentions that it helps him know his voice is worthy of being heard.

And that even if his actual story contains painful paragraphs, he can reframe his story.

And make it matter that those painful moments happened.

Because I know the feeling that my voice is not worthy of being heard, I could hear his voice as he struggled to speak.

I am grateful.

That I recognized him. That I was the little girl who told myself the story that I did.

That I have an opportunity to make it matter that my story happened as it did.

Because I believe that life teaches us in opposites, if I had not known what it was to feel I was not enough to be seen or heard, I would not be the life story listener and writer that I am today. I would not have the honor of crossing paths with voices who struggle to speak.

That I might be able to hand them compassion, worth, purpose, and be a voice for their extraordinary stories. That matter, happening just the way that they have.

Love Blooms in Costco
Jane Gragg Lewis

Love is a shape shifter. One of its very important forms is caring about people we don't know. People we've never seen before, will never see again.

As I walk into Costco, I see a very elderly woman slowly moving behind her cart on her way to the checkout line. For a moment, she and her cart are like a black and white photo in my mind. It reminds me of the black and white scene in *Schindler's List,* with the only spot of color the red coat a little girl is wearing. The pigment in my black and white image is a bright, multi-colored bunch of flowers, the only thing in her cart. I hope she bought them for herself.

After about twenty minutes of "grazing" on snacks and picking up the items on my list, I'm on my way out of Costco. I notice the lady resting on a bench beside the optical department. As I walk past, I realize she's trying without success to stand up. I turn and go back.

Her cart is in front of her knees. She holds the handle with both hands, but every time she attempts to stand, the cart starts to roll away.

I walk over and ask, "Do you want any help?"

Looking rescued, she smiles and says, "That would be nice. Thank you."

I look at the middle-aged man sitting next to her, so close on the short bench that their arms almost touch. He's looking at his cell phone, thumbs busy typing something that I'm sarcastically sure is more important than being a gentleman.

As I hold the cart, the woman tries several times to stand, but I think she isn't making any progress because she's been trying off and on for ten minutes or more, and she's tiring.

I attempt to hold the cart in place while I also hold her left elbow to help her rise, but it just isn't working. The "gentleman" is still busy on his phone. Just as I'm getting ready to not so gently bring him back to the world around him and ask for help, he notices and scrambles to assist.

Oh, the things I want to say!

As the lady and I walk out, she is secure behind her cart and assures me she doesn't need help getting to her car. She pulls a long-stemmed bright pink flower from her bouquet and hands it to me, insisting I take it.

"Thank you for helping me," she says, and gifts me with a smile of appreciation.

"It was my privilege," I say. "You *really* don't need to give me anything."

"Yes, I do," she tells me.

EMPATHY: THE RIPPLE EFFECT
Julie Ryan McGue

One of the questions I often field about my adoption search and reunion experience is how I coped with the devastating denial of my birth mother and the subsequent dismissal by my birth father. I always respond by talking about Catholic Charities, the agency that facilitated my closed adoption in 1959, and the institutional compassion this organization has consistently demonstrated throughout the course of my life. Empathy has a ripple effect. It allows us to feel supported, offers hope, and paves the way to forgiveness and healing.

Decades ago, Catholic Charities instituted a firm policy of placing children from a multiple birth pregnancy into the same adoptive family. By strictly adhering to this guideline, the agency honored the attachment that existed between my sister and me before we were born. It also validated our belonging to one another and reinforced a unique relationship, which has proven integral to our formation of identity. The bond I share with my twin blossomed during our formative years, and as we enter middle age, our connection is strong and true. Our relationship has always been unique, tight, and complicated. We finish each other's thoughts, communicate most effectively nonverbally, and often appear in social settings with similar outfits. We do not just get each other—it is as if we are stitched into the same skin.

In 2008, when I learned I needed a breast biopsy, my sister was my first phone call. We decided it was time to research our adoption and gather family medical history. Together we launched an adoption search that consumed five years. At each juncture, we discussed options and decided upon next steps. She boosted me when I hesitated, doubted, or dipped into the gloom of disappointment. When we hit a milestone, we cheered the glorious achievement together. Without my twin sister, I am not me. Without her, my life journey would be a story less than half-told. And without her holding my hand as we crossed the finish line of our adoption search, the taste of victory would have been bitter, not honey sweet.

The incredible compassion demonstrated by Catholic Charities didn't stop with their insistence on adopting my sister and me into the same family. Through its Post-Adoption Services Department, the organization continues to minister to me with respect to adoption related issues like identity, belonging, rejection, betrayal, and loss. During our five-year adoption search and reunion process, I met quarterly with a support group made up of the adoption constellation: fellow adoptees, birth parents, adoptive parents, siblings, and significant others. Meeting regularly with this group introduced me to the diverse perspectives of others within the adoption world. I came to have empathy for the unique experience of birth parents, and for the challenges adoptive parents face in parenting. Much like the strength I draw from the relationship with my twin sister, my post adoption adult life has been enriched by peer support.

This condensed excerpt from my memoir, *Twice a Daughter: A Search for Identity, Family, and Belonging* describes my first post-adoption support group meeting:

> "The format of the meeting was simple. After signing in, we went around the U-shaped conference table and stated our name, disclosed whether we were an adoptee, birth parent, or adoptive parent, and then we shared where we were in the search and reunion process. If we brought someone with us, we introduced them.
>
> For the icebreaker piece, the moderator asked that we offer a response to this question: "If you could say one thing to the family member you seek, what would that be?"
>
> Ethnically and racially diverse, the group members ran the spectrum in age from thirty-somethings to seventy-year-olds. Except for two birth mothers, the rest were adult adoptees, and all but three were women. The common thread: Catholic Charities had facilitated everyone's adoption.
>
> More than half of us were waiting to hear back from a birth parent or birth daughter/son. From my experience of waiting weeks for my birth mom to answer my (first) outreach, I knew

how excruciating passing the time could be. A woman, I guessed her to be in her late thirties, had been anticipating a response from her birth mother for over a year. When she broke down in sobs during her introduction, the Kleenex box at the center of the table shot over to her like a hockey puck.

One of the birth mothers and a female adoptee shared their reunion stories. Both glowed like someone who'd recently fallen in love. They passed around photos of themselves beaming, wrapped in tight embraces with their newfound relatives. To the group's credit, each of us ogled at how much the searchers resembled their child or parent, and each attendee professed such joy and support for the searcher that I wondered why I'd delayed in joining such a compassionate crowd.

When it was my turn to talk, I clasped my sweaty hands tightly in my lap. "I'm Julie. This is my first meeting. I'm an adoptee." I tried to make eye contact with the people across the table. "I also happen to be a twin. Thanks to Catholic Charities' policy of keeping twins together, my sister and I were adopted into the same family." I smiled at our moderator, and then I looked down at the tabletop. "Due to health concerns, I began the search for my birth mother last year. Last month, I learned that she didn't want to connect with us. I'm hoping she'll change her mind someday." When I glanced up, I caught the Kleenex box just in time.

The moderator jumped in. "And Julie, how would you answer the icebreaker question?"

The tissue balled up in my palm. I'd thought hard about this when the others spoke. The angry-rejected-adoptee-me, the one I'd been working hard at controlling these days, wanted to ask my birth mom: how could she look herself in the mirror every day, she who gave up not one, but two daughters, and rejected both of us. Twice. The person-that-was-me-before-this-adoption-search, the one I was desperately trying to reclaim 24/7, chose a different response to offer the group. "I would ask her if she has thought of my sister and me throughout her life, and if she ever wondered what had happened to us."

Due to COVID, my Catholic Charities post-adoption support group now meets virtually rather than in-person. Through this safe space, I have made lifelong friends, people with whom I shared an instant connection due to our shared experience. This format put me in conversation with birth mothers who provided valuable insights into the behavior and emotions of my own birth mother. Seeing adoption through her eyes gave me compassion for her role as an unwed mother in the 1950s. Because of my continued involvement in this group, I'm a fierce advocate for peer support.

Recently, I was a guest speaker on a panel of writers. During the Q&A portion, the question came up of where we find courage and resiliency. I mentioned my relationship with my sister and my reliance on the Catholic Charities support group. A woman, who I will call Sara, raised her hand in the chat. She was joining us from Australia, which meant she had risen at dawn to connect to the Zoom meeting.

Sara shared that she is a birth mom and that she had read my memoir. Twice. Upon finishing it the first time, Sara had wept. My story had awakened complicated, suppressed thoughts and emotions. Reading the book had provided steps for Sara to begin to heal from the trauma of her adoption loss.

To our cozy virtual group, Sara said, "When I got to the chapter in *Twice a Daughter* about the support group meeting, I realized I needed peer support. Right away. I hadn't known such therapy groups existed for women like me." Through her tears, Sara thanked me for my story.

Many of us struggle from the effects of our lived experiences. To cope, accept, and heal from all that life throws our way, there are many benefits to be drawn from the support of like-minded peers, counselors, and therapists. Seeing through others' eyes fosters self-improvement. It enables relationships to gain momentum. Receiving compassion and offering empathy is not just a gift we offer to ourselves and others. The ripple effect is felt within the family unit, the community, and beyond.

EMPATHETIC LAUGHING EYES
Christy-Holly Piszkiewicz

I really needed to find a bathroom after landing in Ecuador. I couldn't use the lavatory on the small plane.

Gazing at a young woman standing near the bathrooms in an airport maintenance uniform, I walked toward her. She looked up to see a heavyset older woman in a bright summer dress. What made her stare were the huge plaster casts on my arms.

I swallowed my pride and asked this lady to help me.

"*Por favor,*" I started in my limited Spanish. Then, startled, she followed me into a women's bathroom.

"*Te importante,*" I squeaked, while trying to speak Spanish. "*Gracias.*"

She accompanied me into a stall, where she understood she was to pull down my underwear and helped me sit on the commode.

Ahh. Relief!

Red-faced at this intimate act done by a stranger, we locked eyes. With a bit of laughter and a sisterly look, she helped me get up, pulled my panties over my very ample hips, and ensured my dress was lying down. As I exited the bathroom saying, "*Gracias,*" she was washing her hands, and I saw a reflection—with a "Boy, do I have a story to tell at the dinner table" look.

Stopping in Panama City, again with no available family toilet, I approached a female security guard to help me in my distress. It took a bit longer to mime what I needed her for. At this point, I was past the "dancing stage" and needed to go. Luckily, as she pulled down my pants, I could sit down in time. Having her help me up was an ordeal. But soon I was up, pantsed, and she motioned me to go first to wash my hands. It was comical since I only had fingertips protruding from my casts.

I was so grateful for this woman in my life as I walked back to my waiting husband. He felt so sad that he couldn't help me. There are accessible bathroom stalls in the women's lavatory, but he couldn't assist me in them.

The next stop was the airport in New Jersey, and yes, you guessed it, no family bathroom. But at least I could converse in English. I found myself gravitating toward a mature woman, asking her to help me. I told her of my misadventures—how, while on a lava island, my feet found a rare hole trying to get my balance, and I pitched forward into another irregular hole! I had broken both of my radius bones.

She helped me, and once again, I had to bury my pride to allow a stranger to pull down my pants. Filled with gratitude, I looked up and told her how lucky I was to have her help me. "Yes, of course," she remarked, "but I am thankful you only had to urinate."

At our last stop, the Cincinnati airport, I was so appreciative that it had a family bathroom where my husband could help me use the toilet.

Empathetic women that I met on the spot respectfully assisted me when I needed their help. Their compassion toward me will always fill a warm part of my heart.

HERSHEY, THE MAN
Marlene B. Samuels

"Incredible, I can still remember the G.I.'s name was James! So compassionate, handsome, but a very shy soldier. He was an African-American from Georgia, who I now realize was just a kid. I'll bet until the war, he'd probably never before been away from home." Seren, my mom reminisces. "He was the G.I. who carried me out of Dachau, not that carrying me was any big deal because I weighed only sixty-five pounds, so at five-foot-two, I wasn't much to manage." She smiles trying to add levity to what, otherwise, is a terrifying history.

"Mom, that's horrible." I say.

"Not really, Marlene. My story sounds sad to you but it does have a happy outcome, right? I'm here, you're here, and so is your brother."

"Tell me more," I say. I've heard her stories numerous times yet they always sound fresh.

"James became that kid who sat on a rickety stool next to my hospital cot every single week, monitoring me as though I was some broken-winged sparrow he'd rescued. During his visits, I agonized how I might speed up my recovery. He kept a close watch, the way the savior of that damaged bird might wait and pray for it to take flight. James hoped for such signs before he had to return to the U.S.A.

"You know, I really lived a happy life in Romania until those horrible things started happening to us Jews. Could anyone have imagined people could commit such evils against other people?" my mother asks. When she begins any of her stories, her words cease for a few seconds while emotions evoked by her memories play on her face. I know she's entering her secret and terrifying memory place—one few understand nor would care to. Her breath becomes labored as though a delicate fish bone has gotten lodged in her throat. It's obvious to me that recounting her experiences has lodged in her heart, not her throat.

Regaining her composure, Mom focuses upon the empathy and compassion she was shown, delighting in memories of those experiences. "I was taken to a Red Cross Hospital and Rehabilitation Center organized by the Americans to deal with us. We were Dachau survivors, liberated by American G.I.'s. I'll never forget how cute they were, but the doctors—they were something else!" A smile crosses her lips. For a few seconds, she's back in her twenties. "Those doctors spent every minute of every hour for six months pulling me back into life. Honestly, I haven't a clue when they slept!

"I finally met him the at the hospital when I regained consciousness."

Mom refers to the World War II years when she was in Dachau as the lost years. "My greatest misfortune was being a Jew in Hitler's Europe, a time that spawned colossal madness and tragedy." She adds, "Decades have passed since then, but I still struggle to understand how those horrors happened to us. It's shocking that even today so many people refuse to believe human beings committed such evils against other humans—except I witnessed them and experienced them first hand!" She nods as if following a hypnotist's pendulum.

"You know that by 1945, I was anything but the enthusiastic tourist I'd always been before the war. Instead, I'd become a liberated concentration-camp survivor with nothing but my life. The American soldiers found us still alive in the camp, but it was James who found me. They took us to that Red Cross hospital in Bavaria, most of us more dead than alive."

I'd heard about James often, knew the story's sequence, yet whenever I hear it, the conversations are unfamiliar to me. Mom pretends she's never before told me this story.

"James showed up to visit every week, bringing me all the Hershey chocolate bars that were packed inside his G.I. meal boxes. I was extremely malnourished," she explains, "suffering with typhus, dysentery, multiple fractures and skin ulcers." Her eyes tear as she recalls her condition. "None of us could eat anything, but if I'd been able to, it definitely would have been chocolate."

"Did you ever eat them?" I ask. "I can't imagine I'd have been able to resist!"

"I couldn't eat a thing, but didn't need to. I still enjoyed them and especially James visiting me. Imagine, he brought so many Hershey bars, they created a teetering tower on my nightstand. They actually smelled more chocolaty to me than chocolate now does."

"Imagine, that cute guy sat with me every single week. I was twenty-seven and still bald from when the Nazis had shaved my head." My blond-haired resilient mother continues, "Whenever I saw James enter our ward and head towards my cot, I'd call out in my weak voice, 'James, good to see you!' But my English was awful. I pronounced the few English words I did know with a Romanian accent ten times heavier than it is now!"

In short order, the G.I. acquired a new name. Among his fellow soldiers, doctors, nurses and patients, he became known as "Hershey." He continued to visit Seren, his arms always loaded with Hershey bars he'd saved from his and his friends' rations.

"Then, on the first Thursday of November," her eyes glisten with memories, "Hershey arrived one hour early and not in uniform. He was dressed in 'civvies' looking even handsomer—movie star handsome. How hadn't I noticed sooner? And in his arms stacked to his chin, were Hershey chocolate bars!"

"Why was he so dressed up?" I ask, although I know from prior tellings.

"The second I saw him I knew, but pretended I didn't. Honestly, I just sensed it. He had a pretend-smile as if he'd been crying but wanted to look happy for me. You know that look?"

I nod so she'll continue. "He walked slowly, talking all the way to my cot," she says, "as if to get out what it was he came to tell me as quickly as possible. Then he sat down, stared into my eyes and said it. 'I came to say goodbye, Seren.' Hershey actually used my name. I was so surprised he even knew it!"

My mother smiles, describing her first happiness after unimaginable sorrows. " 'Tomorrow we're heading home.' Hershey told me. 'They promised our unit we'd be home for Thanksgiving.'

Poor kid. He just sat on that hard stool as tears poured down his smooth brown cheeks, so smooth like he'd just shaved."

"Did you celebrate Thanksgiving in Romania?" I ask.

"You kidding? I'd never even heard of it. To Hershey I said, 'This word - I don't know.' His answer surprised me.

"'You definitely do!' then he changed the subject to keep our last hour together happy. I remember he pointed to the top of my head. 'Wow, your hair's growing back!' Little blond hairs were popping out all over my scalp like grass-seedlings."

Maybe Mom smiled at him, proud of her gradual transformation back into the beauty she'd been before the war. "'Yes, see?' I asked Hershey. I remember bending my head forward to give him a better look, like I was some French model showing him the latest hairstyle. We both laughed but I think that was the first time in years I'd laughed."

"'Seren, don't eat all that chocolate alone or you might get even fatter than you are now, right? Doc says you've gotten to a whopping eighty-eight pounds.' I really did giggle when he said that, but then he started crying again. We were so desperate to communicate that we spoke in German, the only language we both knew, but hated."

That last conversation Mom recounts always catches me unprepared. "You know something?" Hershey asked, "I never knew there were blond-haired, blue-eyed Jews until I met you, Seren."

"And you know something else? I never knew there were dark-eyed, brown-skinned American G.I.'s until I met you, James."

I have to wonder whether Hershey's eyes released even more tears.

"Seren, you've changed my life forever. I'll never forget you!"

"And Hershey, you saved my life. I'll always remember you!"

That first week of November, 1945, was the last time my mother ever saw Hershey. And the second week of November, 1945, was the first week of her second life.

Sun Sets on a Sufi
Monique S. Simón

Looking out my kitchen window
Waiting for the sun to set
For a Sufi
Observing Ramadan
On the day I have made a feast
To celebrate a joyous occasion

He has joined me here
Since he is my brother
Kinned to me by our longtime friendship
"7:47" he announces
He smiles up at me
I receive his smile with my own
"Have some of the mushroom rice," I insist, as if he were not
    already headed in that direction

I have waited with him for over an hour

I touch his back as we sit and join the others
Already feasting at the dining table
He touches my arm
I feel his warmth, imagining that my love has reached his palate
I too eat
And know the joy of waiting

I discover that patience has a taste

I eat
Delighted
That sun sets on many a Sufi

EMPATHY IN THE TIME OF COVID
Jo-Ann Vega

When I look up empathy in a thesaurus, I'm struck by what I find. Empathy, compassion and understanding, requires three things: affinity, cognitive ability, and personality characteristics. The combination draws one to concerted action on behalf of intimates, associates, and strangers. Empathy originates from an internal knowing, a recognition of need in others *and* self that seeks and is able to help, while honoring the recipient's dignity.

Crises bring out the best and worst in people. Empathy doesn't require a crisis, but it certainly helps during one. I'd like to share a personal encounter with a sudden life-threatening illness during the pandemic. I share this to demonstrate that even in times of personal crisis, there are life-affirming opportunities to offer empathy to others. These unplanned encounters root and spread the seeds of empathy.

During the height of COVID hospitalizations and deaths, after a week of stubbornly trying to manage severe abdominal pain, I reluctantly went to the ER in the local community hospital. After hours of testing, two doctors with long faces entered the treatment room. I knew, before a word was spoken, the news was not good. The first said, "You must be strong! You look better than your CAT scan. You have a massive infection in your colon." Without prompting, the second doctor then offered his assessment, "If I operate today I can't make any promises. You could die or come out with a bag."

I was admitted in the late afternoon, wheeled into a semi-private room, and helped into a hospital bed—a truly amazing piece of technology that was to become home for five days—by two nurses, who were scarcely recognizable in their COVID garb. The only way to recognize the staff, masked and gloved and with heads covered, was to compare the picture on the prominent name tag on their lab coats or gowns to the person's eyes, a narrow slit a few inches wide above the midline of the nose to the eyebrows. It wasn't a comforting sight. All personnel kept their distance.

Despite the pain and the ER docs' sobering visit, I was conscious of my surroundings. I noted the curtain was drawn to separate the other half of the room, where the TV was blasting, medical equipment was beeping, and a loud public phone conversation was taking place.

It didn't take long to realize my roommate also had serious medical issues, a new smart phone she could not operate, and needed help she did not seem able to marshal herself. As long as I can remember, I've been drawn to helping those in need. I am incapable of keeping it to social niceties.

The incessant noise was painful. It gradually dawned on me I was being monitored for sepsis. After several unsuccessful attempts to secure help to stop the beeping from the medical equipment, I asked for earplugs and an eye mask to help me shut out the light, noise, and movement. The room, close to H E L P at the end of a hallway leading to the nurses' station, which was the hub of the floor, was further evidence of the seriousness of our conditions.

The curtain stayed closed the first day. My roommate and I didn't speak to each other; we heard each other's interactions with hospital employees. I don't recall the exact moment I pulled back the curtain on my return from an escorted visit to the bathroom. "Hello, my name is J. Is it okay if we leave the curtain open for a while?" G introduced herself through her mask and agreed.

On the second or third day, I heard a doctor tell G there were additional concerns. Each day, when asked directly how she felt, her reply was, "Okay." He would follow with, "Do you want to go home?" G would answer, "Not yet."

G's condition was worsening and she literally had no one to advocate for her. Her adult children called every day and were, to put it politely, more interested in their lives than their mother's medical status. It was painful to hear their private communications. I'd already intervened on G's behalf several times. She seemed to like that I offered help. We'd been talking a bit since I pulled the curtain back. We were different, almost polar opposites.

The next time G's doctor arrived, I greeted him and asked if he would take a closer look at G, as she wasn't feeling any better. The litany of her medical issues was numerous. On his subsequent visit the doctor informed G she had developed congestive heart failure from her co-morbidities. Sometime later, a technician came in and explained the condition to G. When it came time to ask questions, G didn't have any.

I couldn't believe what I was hearing. Was G in denial, feeling she could not ask questions, or not knowing which questions to ask? I'm not by nature a gushy person. I'm more likely to offer problem-solving.

After some time passed, I raised my bed, leaned over and asked, "G, do you want to leave the hospital?" Her immediate response: "Yes, when I am well."

I looked at G and chose my words. "G, people don't leave the hospital when they are well. They are either recovering or dead. Staying in the hospital is making you sicker." I hesitated before continuing. "Do you realize you are a very sick woman?" She began to quietly cry.

Later on, I took another chance. "G, I'm sorry you haven't been able to get the phone to work properly. Even with the earplugs, I've heard your private conversations. I don't want to hurt your feelings, but your children don't seem to understand your condition. Would you mind if I said something the next time they call?" G nodded.

I could have ignored the situation and focused on my needs. I did what felt natural. The next time G's children called, I gave each an update on their mother's condition. After their initial shock subsided, each expressed concern and changed their interactions with their mother.

On the day of my discharge, I wasn't sure when I'd be back for surgery or if my body was turning against me. My infection levels had decreased significantly. I was still wearing a drain, which I fervently hoped was not a precursor to a colostomy bag, taking large doses of antibiotics, and beginning to eat. I was uncomfortable and eager to be released.

G took the lead. "I notice that you're quiet and then you start talking and make things happen." I chuckled at the accuracy of her insight. G followed with, "Can you tutor my grandchildren?" It was such an unexpected, honest and emotional appeal. I was touched, recognizing the enormity of her request and apparent trust. I lowered my voice. "G, thank you for recognizing I might help." I sighed loudly. It's not easy to say no, even when the request is a big ask.

I felt for her and turned over in my mind the events of the past days. We shared an intensive and stressful hospitalization during some of the scariest days of the COVID pandemic. With no visitors allowed, we had each other to talk to during a medical storm we each hoped would pass. Under these circumstances, it's not unusual to develop attachments to others we likely would never meet in our daily lives. The intensity of the experience was likely to dissipate outside the hospital, once we returned to our respective lives. I knew this from my training and experience. G knew this as a survivor who had to scratch out a barely modest living.

"G, what you are asking is more than I can do. Thank you for talking with me this week. I hope we both get better. This week may have been our moment though." We chatted for a while and I offered ideas on how to get assistance for her grandchildren.

Now, over a year later, looking back, I'm thankful to have beaten the odds. I hope G did, too. There are boundless opportunities to practice purposeful acts of empathy, regardless of circumstances. Imagine how much this could positively change the country, world, and you.

JUST THIRTY SECONDS
Jude Walsh

I'm a blurter, always have been. I say things before thinking about how people will react. On more than one occasion, after heads swiveled toward me, I realized I had spoken a thought aloud. As most of my thoughts are positive, the blurts usually work out.

On this day, I had just finished an appointment with a pain specialist. I have some arthritis in my feet and hands and her treatments always gave me relief. On the way out, as I walked down the steps, using alternating feet with very little pain, feeling happy and grateful, I noticed a woman at the bottom of the stairs waiting for the elevator. She was older, late 70s I might guess, white hair cropped short in a low-maintenance style. She was leaning heavily on one of those utilitarian tripod canes. She was overweight, kind of pear-shaped, and not very fashionably dressed. She had on loose light blue pants that looked like they had been shortened for her, as they were pretty baggy and wide at the cuff, and an oversized plaid flannel shirt. Her shoulders sloped and her head was down. My heart went out to her.

I said hello and then added the first thing that popped into my mind. "Your shirt, with those soft blues and pinks, is like a breath of springtime." Her face lit up as she glanced at her shirt. "Thank you!" She looked up and smiled at me, "You just made my day." Before my eyes, her posture changed. Her head lifted and her back straightened. Years dropped away as her vigor returned. As I walked away, I replied, "Well, I am happy I could do that."

She didn't see the tears in my eyes. That simple, heartfelt, blurted compliment *made her day*. I'd felt her energy shift as she looked at her shirt through new eyes. I was humbled that a few words, a simple observation, changed her outlook. My friends are always laughing about the way I talk to everybody. "You've never met a stranger, have you, Jude?" I admit I love people and I love connecting, even if just for a few seconds. I look for reasons to give a compliment. My connection to this sweet woman brightened her day. Her response to me reminded me of the power kind words have. Reminded me to just go ahead and speak the thoughts as they come to me. She made *my* day, too.

My words made her happy. She saw herself through the eyes of a stranger and liked what she saw. Her response touched me, lifted me up, and encouraged me to go ahead and keep on blurting out my thoughts. To give the compliment I am thinking. This thirty-second exchange affected us both. I am officially giving myself permission to blurt away.

SAUERKRAUT, PECAN PIES, AND TANNING BEDS
Christina M. Wells

I was trying to squash cabbage and salt into a large trashcan designated for that purpose. "You need to push harder," my wife Jen's grandfather said. "Put your whole body weight into it." We were in Central Pennsylvania making sauerkraut, and I was taking orders from a very old man who somehow was stronger than I was. I simultaneously searched for the door and thought I would never eat sauerkraut again.

"You're lucky," Bill said. "When I first met them, they were slaughtering pigs." He walked by casually with a book. Bill, my father-in-law, had learned to make himself scarce at his in-laws' house. As a retired investigative reporter and humor columnist who had used his family for material, he wasn't the deer-hunting, farming, flannel-shirt type. He went out for chicken and waffles with the best of them, but he wasn't a Central Pennsylvanian. He was a city boy from Erie.

I wasn't always entirely sure Jen's grandparents knew who I was. They hadn't gone to the wedding, and we never really talked about how I was always at family gatherings. Fortunately, there wasn't this awkward silence with my in-laws, Bill and Aimee. They looked at my hazing ritual as pretty standard for an in-law.

Sometimes we wake up to realize we have family in places where we never imagined in our early years. On the surface, they are vastly different from us. Past the surface, they may be inexplicably familiar.

When we first met, there was a large family gathering at a place called Good Wil's. It was shortly before Christmas, and everyone had started eating when Jen and I arrived. In spite of how the entire meal looked like a set-up for an antacid ad, it wasn't too hard to be there. No one made me call the Hogs (I'm from Arkansas, you know), and nobody seemed like they were going to take out a Bible and pray over us. It was successful.

Later, Bill decided that he would call me Erica for a good part of an evening, even though he knew better (although I'm not sure he could remember my actual name). "But you look like an Erica," he said. "Couldn't Erica have been your name at some point?"

I'm not sure Bill initially got it when Jen and I decided to get married, but he did something that many people wouldn't have done under similar circumstances: he did research. He must have been in the advanced class, because by the time we actually got married, he stood with my father while they made toasts to us at our wedding reception, and he made a humdinger of a mimosa toast before brunch that people still remember. I'm sure it didn't hurt that he actually liked me. But he took the time to see what it might be like to be in our situation, and our marriage got to be like anybody's marriage.

We even adopted our own pastime. In the years that followed, Jen and Aimee decided to watch those contemporary holiday movies on cable, the ones that have a pretty clear direction. Bill and I sometimes created our own dialogue, sort of like that old show, "Mystery Science Theater." This could go on to the point where Aimee begged us to stop and we acted like we would. We didn't always.

Bill had a secondary pastime of asking me if I'd make him a pecan pie. I confessed that the recipe came from the Karo syrup bottle, but it didn't matter. Thanksgiving, Christmas, or mid-July, he always thought I should be making a pecan pie, since he'd discovered that I could, in fact, make a good pecan pie.

Later, when I started writing more and sending it out, he expressed interest in what I was doing. "Can I read something sometime?" he would say. He asked me about my projects, and when I quit my job as a college professor, he didn't have the fit over money that a lot of people would have had. "Tell Christina I'm proud she's following her dreams," he told Jen one night on the phone. At this point, he was in a lot of pain. He'd had innumerable back surgeries and had been losing weight mysteriously even though he ate chocolates, cookies, and peppermint patties on a regular basis.

We later found that he had leukemia, a belated parting gift from Agent Orange and the Vietnam War, where he'd worked in counterintelligence. None of us really knew what to say. That "not knowing what to say" carried some of us all the way to the knowledge he had entered Stage 4.

Jen and I were planning on going to New York for a weekend to stay at the Algonquin, the old stomping grounds of Dorothy Parker and her circle. We thought of going to see a show some friends had seen, and we talked about meeting a friend who lives in Brooklyn.

Then something hit me, and it hit Jen at the same time. We could go to New York sometime soon, but we really wanted to see Bill sooner. We might have had a couple of years without much travel, courtesy a global pandemic. We also didn't know how long Stage 4 would be, for his type of leukemia, or what it would mean if we waited to see him at our niece's graduation.

So we went to Erie. We filled up the Subaru (yeah, I know—stereotype) and buckled in our dog, Angus (see earlier parenthetical). We went on our way, taking the Turnpike at Breezewood, the way we always do when going to western PA.

That weekend, I learned there were few limits to the sense of humor that Bill and I somehow manage to share, though he is a Boomer straight guy and I am a Gen X lesbian. I saw him at the head of the table one morning, eating his cereal and taking an awfully long time with the obituaries. I read them at home, and something suddenly occurred to me. Under most circumstances, it wouldn't be the kind of thing to share with someone who had recently been to a funeral home to make his own arrangements. "Hey, Bill. I read an obituary in the *Washington Post* where one of the dead guy's hobbies was reading the obituaries."

"There's some interesting stuff in them," he said, laughing. He went back to reading, trying to put a more serious look on his face. I exhaled. Right in the middle of that story, I wasn't sure it was a good idea. But somehow it was.

I should have known. The night before, we had sat around for a rousing reading of the warnings about his chemo drug, you know, as one does when someone in the living room has Stage 4 anything.

I was coming back from the bathroom when I heard Bill say, loudly, "But I've always wanted to carry a child!"

"I have to tell you that that's a really interesting thing to hear on the way into a room," I said.

"I'll never breastfeed!" Bill said. Now that he knew we were all listening, he was on a roll.

"I want to read them when you're done," I said to Jen.

A moment later, I skimmed through the list. "Bill, it says here that you aren't supposed to go to a tanning bed while on this medication. How many people do you think feel like you feel and go to a tanning bed?" The conversation pretty much went downhill from there.

The next day, after Bill read the obituaries, Jen and I prepared to leave. We were doing last minute hugs and trying to get our dog's act together. I hugged Bill. Then I said, "Don't go to any tanning beds."

"No tanning beds. Yes." I saw him smile to himself as I walked down the hall with Jen to the car outside.

My father-in-law's humor columns ended before I was officially a part of the family. They featured the missteps and absurdities of the family, and sometimes the warmth and celebration. I have long wanted to look at him the same way he does the rest of us—with the wit and candor of someone paying very close attention. He is, much like the rest of us, a real character in mid-story.

HOW IT COULD BE

Married to the U.S. Disabled Ski Team – Three Moments of Perspective
Kathie Arcide

One

I was married to the U.S. Disabled Ski Team for thirteen years.

I never met such a wonderful bunch of guys. They were also irreverent, as evidenced in their pet names for each other. There was Wheelie, Flipper, Stumpy, Gimpy, Half-Matt, and my husband, Blinky. I'll let you guess what kind of disability each loving, but cheeky, name represents.

Over the years, I got to see Team USAble compete in several events, and visited them at training camps in spectacular locations, like Park City, Utah, and West Yellowstone, Montana.

My favorite competition was a six-stage relay race in Bellingham, Washington. The event, called the Ski to Sea, started high up on Mount Baker, which holds the record for highest annual snowfall of any resort in the world. The relay ends thirty miles away down in Bellingham Bay.

Team USAble refused to be put into the Run for Fun category, not wanting to be given special privileges because of their disabilities. They had to fight to be accepted into the Competitive category. They wanted to win, not because they were good despite their limitations, but because they were damn good athletes!

The legs of the race were Cross Country Skiing (Flipper), Downhill Skiing (Wheelie), Running down the mountain road seven miles (Blinky), twenty miles on a Road Bike (Half-Matt), Canoeing down a river (Stumpy), Cyclocross Biking (Gimpy), and ending with Sea Kayaking across the bay (Wheelie).

Our Anchor, AKA "Wheelie," with his gymnast's upper body strength, kayaked five miles across Bellingham Bay to get the team's baton to the finish line.

To complete this relay course, the final contestant, exhausted, often with legs asleep, had to scramble onto the rocky shore, run up a hill, and ring the famous victory bell—a familiar sound, ringing out across the crowd, eliciting cheers and applause with every clang!

No matter how tired that Anchor was, no one on their team was allowed to help.

In their first Ski to Sea relay, Team USAble's final athlete, a double leg-amputee/sit-skier, pulled himself out of his kayak and "gorilla-walked" (that's what they call it) up to that finish line bell, only to find it too high to reach—not something anyone had foreseen.

The rest of the Team, determined to compete as equal athletes, had to stand by, helpless!

Without a thought, and in an act of true sportsmanship, a bunch of recent finish-line-crossers from other teams, ran over and hoisted Wheelie up so he could ring that bell, officially registering Team USAble's finishing time.

Out of over 300 team entries that year, Team USAble came in 27th.

Two

The Cascade Mountain Range in Washington State is beautiful but…

The only time I've been to Europe was to attend the 1992 Winter Paralympics. It was the first time the Paralympics were held concurrently with the regular Olympics, a hard-won victory for disabled athletes.

The Olympics were held that year in Albertville, France. The Para activities were centered twenty miles away, in tiny Tignes, France, a picturesque town nestled deep in a valley in the French Alps.

The Paralympics Opening Ceremony was every bit of what we've come to expect for the Olympics, with all the TV-worthy happenings. Imagine you are sitting in the bleachers, surrounded by beautiful, towering mountain peaks that would make Washington State's Mounts Baker and Rainier curtsy. Each competing country's team, in their designer outfits, strides onto the field in time with music chosen by their country.

Now imagine looking up to see paragliders, one at a time, each with their country's flag as their glider wing, launching off pristine peaks, and gracefully circling the stadium. Perfectly choreographed, as their song ends, and their team completes their arrival march, they each land softly, right in front of the Olympic Rings and Flame.

Our American flag was never more beautiful. As it balleted down onto the field, Queen belted out our country's chosen song, "We are the Champions." I got goosebumps that day from more than the ten-degree weather.

I loved sharing meals with all the athletes in the huge, summer-camp-like dining hall. Guests of the teams (wives, sometimes children) were served last, and at separate tables, but I always sat as close as I could to the American team.

One time I witnessed in action that irreverence I mentioned. It came in the form of an ambush. The team members had an ongoing complaint that none of their trainers, guides or coaches were disabled, not really understanding their team members' individual limitations. So, at one dinner, the training staff was greeted with an organized challenge from the team.

"Pick an athlete, and eat your dinner exactly like they have to."

Wheelchairs appeared. Hands were tied behind backs. Blindfolds secured. And bless their hearts, those coaches went through every step of the meal, experiencing the reality of their guys' lives for the first time.

They made a mess. They stumbled. They dropped stuff. They broke stuff. They embarrassed themselves.

And sometimes, in painful enlightenment, they had no choice but to ask for help.

THREE

My favorite event at the Olympics was after the closing ceremony.

There is a final celebratory dinner, where all the teams from all the countries gather to feast, visit, reminisce, and to participate in a longtime tradition of exchanging personal memorabilia and athletic items with as many other countries' team members as they can. They trade everything—from team buttons and pins to uniforms and equipment. Occasionally, there will even be an informal auction-type sale/trade of something big—not a medal, of course, but I witnessed the polite haggling, mostly through charades and sign language, among a large group of mixed countries, sort of "bidding" on the U.S. Paraglider's wing! I think Denmark got it.

My husband, Joseph, a few tables away from me, was in the middle of one of these treasure exchanges. As an able-bodied person, you learn quickly that none of these world-class athletes like to get uninvited help from anyone, but watching Joseph and the Downhill Skier from Germany try to trade something with each other, it was all I could do to keep my seat.

Joseph had approached the medal-winning German skier to offer him his official U.S. Team ski gloves, and to accept a gift in return. But the German guy kept silently shaking his head, "No."

Thinking maybe the German's silence meant it was perceived as too big a gift, Joseph kept reassuring him it was okay to accept the U.S. ski gloves he was offering, but he could not get the German to take them. I'll say here that Joseph usually hid his blindness well, so the other athlete had no idea Joseph couldn't see all of his emphatic gesturing, or his own held-out gift.

The German continued to offer this blind American guy his goggles.

What Joseph couldn't see is that his co-athlete in this animated exchange had no hands. They had been blown off in a fireworks accident.

Just like when a group of dancers backs away in a circle to give a talented couple space to perform, a crowd had formed around these American and German athletes. They watched silently as these sincere, frustrated, back-and-forth attempts continued.

And not a single person jumped in to explain.

In the end, the blind American guy being offered goggles, points to his eyes and says vigorously, "no danke, no danke, no danke." And the handless guy from Germany, being offered gloves, finally realized the problem.

In an unusually tender gesture for these macho competitors, the German put the stumps of his arms in Joseph's outreached hands.

The room, to a person, erupted in celebration!

Addendum

Just below a medal, the most prized possession of every Winter Olympics athlete is their Team Ski Jacket. That's exactly what this German and American finally ended up exchanging.

You're Special – Words of Empathy
Carol J. Wechsler Blatter

I.

Imagine: "And the award goes to Mr. Rogers in the category of Empathy. Please come to the stage to receive your award." Mr. Rogers slowly walks up several steps to the stage. He is wearing one of the cardigan sweaters he is best known for, this one in light blue. The curtain goes up and twenty children come forward, surround him, and applaud. One of the children gives him a pair of his famous sneakers. An Academy assistant brings out a chair and Mr. Rogers sits down, unties his regular black shoes, takes them off, puts on his gray sneakers, ties them, gets up, and hugs each of the children who have come to honor him.

He goes to the lectern, adjusts the microphone, and says: Dear Members of the Selection Committee of the Academy of the Human Heart, it is an honor to receive this award (then he holds up a commemorative statue bearing his name).

My achievement in the category of Empathy goes to the children, and all the mothers and fathers, and all the hard-working staff at station WQED in Pittsburgh, Pennsylvania, who joined with me to create and sustain Mister Rogers' Neighborhood for many years. They have taught me the meaning of empathy. They have given me many more opportunities to nurture others than I ever could have imagined. (He points to the statue.) This is for all of you here and my TV family and my own family. I have been fortunate to communicate right into all your hearts. That's what empathy is all about.

Fred Rogers used empathic words. "I love you just as you are. You're special."

Whatever your age, whatever your life's stories, he validated all of us. He brought children into his neighborhood, a safe and loving place of love and acceptance, a community where together we support one another. Mr. Rogers translated his fears from childhood, his uncertainties, and his worries, and talked to children—often through puppets. Sometimes he communicated in silence, quiet moments where no one talked, but everyone felt comfortable. His speech was gentle and slow, his mild delivery was impactful. Every child watching TV had the opportunity to grow in self-esteem. Every child heard words of comfort and protection; every child felt loved and appreciated.

II.

I see you're in pain. I am worried about you. I sense something is wrong. I'm here for you. Do you need help?

Empathy is typically a learned behavior, although there may be an inborn capacity for it that needs further development. An empathic person feels someone else's pain, imagines that this could be his or her pain, and responds with care, concern, and compassion. Such a person listens intently to others. Such a person has a heightened sensitivity to where others are coming from. Such a person is often intuitive. Such a person sees, hears, and feels what others see, hear, and feel. Such a person values others. Such a person makes their relationships meaningful and a core part of their lives.

III.

Here are personal examples of the ways our family has shown empathy by reaching out and helping others:

- Participated in hospice training and cared for a hospice patient.
- Resettled Jewish Russians who were permitted to leave.
- Volunteered from our synagogue group to go to the hospital on Christmas day and relieve the Christian volunteers for tasks such as pushing the magazine and candy carts, so they could celebrate their holiday.
- Prepared sandwiches for the homeless.
- Volunteered to help elementary school children with reading.

IV.

Empathy is a necessary tool that we writers use to create complex and compelling characters— characters our readers will identify with. We birth our characters just as mothers give birth to their children. We create characters often struggling to make sense of their lives and the lives of those around them, just as many of us are struggling to make sense of our own lives. An example is the use of empathy in *To Kill a Mockingbird*.

Empathy in *To Kill a Mockingbird*
May 27, 2020, by Essay Writer

Atticus Finch represented a young man of color accused of raping a white girl in the 1930s. Eight decades since then, now in 2022, race is still an issue. There have been multiple episodes of white police officers killing black men. In many past instances, the white officers were not held legally responsible. This changed with the killing of George Floyd, a man of color, who was picked up by police officer Derek Chauvin and two other officers for a report by a store clerk, who suspected Floyd gave him a counterfeit twenty-dollar bill. It was horrifying to watch this officer on TV relentlessly leaning on the neck of George Floyd until he died. Chauvin received a prison sentence of 22.5 years.

Empathy is the ability to share in or understand others' emotions and feelings. It is the term of emotional understanding and a special skill for individuals. This skill requires people to look at things from other people's views. According to Atticus Finch, 'you never really understand a person until you consider things from his point of view…until you climb inside of his skin and walk around in it.' There are many circumstances in this novel where empathy towards others is demonstrated or learned by positive characters such as Atticus, Scout, and Jem.

Fear of the other abounds. For a percentage of people in our country fear of the other continues to escalate into acts of violence. There have been white supremacist marches, one a few years ago in Charlottesville VA, where a woman was killed, had marchers shouting, "Jews will not replace us." The Anti-Defamation League has reported recent increasing incidents of anti-Semitism. Episodes of violence against Asian-Americans have risen. How do we understand this escalation of hatred toward others? For one, ignorance. Misinformation and disinformation has escalated, often perpetuated on social media. For another, hating others and acting out this hatred elevates insecure people, who blame others for their alienation and lack of success. For another, learning to hate can be taught in families. I'm reminded of the following song in the play and movie, "South Pacific":

> "YOU'VE GOT TO BE CAREFULLY TAUGHT"
> You've got to be taught to hate and fear,
> You've got to be taught from year to year,
> It's got to be drummed in your dear little ear—
> You've got to be carefully taught!"

V.

"Reach out and touch someone" was an AT&T marketing success several years ago. Why did it work? Because AT&T harnessed words of universality. It touched the innate human hunger to be close to someone else and to know that someone else wants to be close to us. The phone was, and still is, a vehicle for talking with a loved one, a family member, a good friend, or a shut-in neighbor: "How are you? I am thinking about you."

Daily Life In Our Digital Age
Cynthia F. Davidson

Pushing the vacuum cleaner across the living room carpet this afternoon, I suddenly burst into tears. How hopeless my busy efforts are. How dumb this useless machine when pitted against the tanks and AR-15s. Where is the equipment we actually need, for real work, to clean up the world's massive messes?

While I try to tidy up my Rhode Island home, displaced people starve in refugee camps, and someone plans the next mass-shooting spree, or aims a Russian artillery strike. Yet if I stop, and sit down to grieve the eight-year-olds gunned down in their Uvalde classroom this week, or reread the obituary of my high school classmate, or commiserate with shell-shocked Ukrainians staring at their pulverized apartments, I may never leave my couch.

Nothing quite opens your eyes, or breaks your heart, like being online each day. In our Digital Age we peer through so many pairs of eyes. During the Agrarian, Industrial, and Information Ages, we did not have all these perspectives, nor the continuous feedback loop. Now, it's 360 degrees of tragedy, along with the terrible consequences of wars, climate change, and the violent refusals to coexist in peace. Although I developed a tolerance for disaster when working at CBS News, the Digital Age is different. Now it's personal. The distances have disappeared. The names confront us and demand action.

This morning, on Facebook, I responded to Naila in Pakistan, lamenting the latest floods. And saw Belgian-born Eryk's pictures of poppies blooming in Denmark, alongside his exhortations to carry extra bottles of water to share with the homeless during this summer of record heat in Las Vegas where he lives. Mary in Massachusetts is recovering from a brain bleed. Friend Henry just received a serious diagnosis. Sue got a visit from her grandkids. Rolando had a birthday. A pal in Florida is scheduled for knee replacement surgery… The pleas for prayers, good vibes and positive energy are balanced, somewhat, by the happier announcements—'aced my nursing exam,' held my 'first great-grandchild,' 'got that job'—and cancer survivor updates. These arrive in my News Feed sandwiched between book reveals, birthday notices, wedding pix, sobriety anniversaries and funerals.

The bulk of these messages stream in from people who've never physically met the non-digital me. Even though I've been online for over a dozen years already, this is new ground we're creating as the first generation to have these communication tools. Their powers demand adjustments. Never have humans had to synthesize this much content and digest 360 degrees' worth of comments and criticisms. Countless disagreements swirled in with all the kindred spirit kudos.

Because we can, I have kept up with people met briefly in person, like retired pastor Elizabeth Bowen. During an interminable delay on an Amtrak train to Boston several years ago, she struck up a conversation. And sadly, she became the first person I knew to die from COVID. After two-years-plus living with SARS-CoV-2 and its variants, my husband, son, and daughter have had it and a million Americans have been lost, along with millions more overseas. In our Digital Age these numbers translate into Friends, friends of Friends, and their relatives on social media pages.

I am far more sentimental than previously suspected. A prime coping mechanism is my social media interaction, activism, and education. But what's most difficult is dealing with the deceased, especially when Facebook prompts me to delete previous Friends to make room for the new requests.

Stubbornly, I keep visiting the legacy pages of people like Julie de Forest, world traveler and former flight attendant. Spunky, sassy, and well informed, we connected over our resistance to Trump. A widow whose pilot partner died from a rare cancer, she was caring for her mom. She was sure they'd both had COVID before it had a name. They died four months apart, before she had the satisfaction of seeing that one-term president lose his bid for reelection. Her Friends still stop by her page to assure her spirit "the Good Fight continues."

Others include Mika and Deedee, two trans women Friends, whose life experiences, concern for others, and resilient humor has cheered me on. And Dana, my brave gay friend since elementary school in Saudi Arabia, who couldn't do it anymore. Devorah Winegarten, who wrote *There's Jews in Texas?* and embodied the word *chutzpah*. From her hospital bed, she had her handfasting ceremony. Tammy and Glenda, ceremonial sisters, stricken too soon and gone…

As I write this, we are only halfway through 2022 and I shudder to imagine what's next. How could we survive the loneliness of lockdowns and quarantines during this pandemic, or send kids to school online, if we weren't in the Digital Age? My kids have watched who's gone to bat for them during the latest legislative crises, too, as reproductive rights, guaranteed for the last fifty years, have been snatched away by justices who lied during their Supreme Court confirmation hearings. For the first time in history, the next generation can clearly see who's fighting for fairness, and the future, along with who is opting out.

I wonder what I'd be thinking if I hadn't met Gulia K. online years ago. An immigrant from the old Soviet Union, she and Mikhail provide the kind of context you can only get from people who grew up speaking Russian. And Nadin B. in Ukraine tonight is privy to military bloggers reporting that the Russian army has just missed its first pay period.

I get back up and switch on my vacuum cleaner, recalling the power of phones and laptops when hitched to global platforms. These are the machines we need to fix the world. For the first time in history, Russian moms went on social media to plead for news about their sons when their commanders ignored their desperate calls. Putin sent their boys into Ukraine without declaring war before ordering them to invade. Some conscripts ran out of ammo, fuel and food, and abandoned their armored vehicles. Ukrainian moms responded to their Russian counterparts. They gave the boys their phones to call home and fed them before sending them back to the border.

Don't underestimate the power of social media in our Digital Age. May the moms take over.

THE POOR LITTLE MATCHSTICK GIRL
Sara Etgen-Baker

When Henry Buhler sold all but ten acres of his massive farmland, a developer bought it, converting it into a subdivision with row upon row of two-bedroom, cracker box houses built to attract young couples, who were beginning their families. Within a few short years, the blue-collar neighborhood was teeming with children whose parents were poor and nomadic, renting the cheap houses for only a short period of time. Our neighborhood quickly became a revolving door, with vagabond families moving in and out every three to six months.

Their children freely roamed neighborhood streets, drawn to our home like iron shavings to a magnet, showing up in our front yard seemingly from nowhere and typically around mealtime. They joined us in whatever game my brothers and I were playing that day. When the game ended, Mother emerged from the house, giving them a brown paper sack with a peanut butter sandwich and some of her homemade cookies. She occasionally outfitted some of them in shoes and clothes we'd outgrown and gave them toys we'd discarded.

"I don't understand why you take care of all these ragamuffin children. You can barely feed and clothe your own!" Grammy often complained.

"We'll manage," was Mother's cheerful response.

"You can't possible know if you're making a difference."

"You're right," she said. "I don't know, but I was a ragamuffin myself and know first-hand what it feels like to wear ill-fitting, dirty clothes and go to bed with my tummy aching from hunger, wondering when I might eat again. So I choose to be empathetic, kind, and compassionate in these children's lives today and to rely on something bigger than me to make a difference down the road."

Deanna was once such a ragamuffin little girl, who wandered into our front yard one bitterly cold January afternoon, where my brothers and I were playing a winter version of dodgeball using snowballs. She was the epitome of a ragamuffin—a malnourished little girl roughly my age, wearing a tattered dress and worn-out old shoes too big for her feet. She was coatless, and her small hands were gloveless, numb and slightly red from being exposed to the cold. Her face was grimy and bore the most woeful look—a look that reminded me of Hans

Christian Andersen's poor little matchstick girl. When I approached her she looked as if she was on the verge of crying, and I wondered if she dared not go home because she'd not sold any matches.

Deanna was sweet, though, and we quickly became friends, eating lunch together at school and jumping rope with one another during recess. After school, we walked home together then sat on my front porch finishing our homework, playing card games and checkers, and cutting out clothes for our paper dolls.

"I don't think Deanna has toys at her house," Mother casually mentioned one day. "Just imagine how lonely and boring that must be for her," she went on, nudging me to put myself in Deanna's shoes. "Maybe you could give her one of your dolls." I did, of course, because I couldn't conceive of not having a doll to sleep with at night.

Just before my elementary school's annual father-daughter banquet, Mother took me aside. "Not every little girl's father is like yours. Deanna's daddy is a damaged man whose soul is broken. When a man's soul is broken, he's full of anger—hurtful anger that comes out in what he says and does. Imagine living with a daddy like that," she said, again asking me again to place myself in Deanna's shoes. "How would you feel about sharing your daddy with her on the night of the father-daughter banquet?"

Sharing my dolls was one thing, but sharing my daddy? That was something entirely different! I reluctantly agreed, harboring a little childhood resentment. On the night of the banquet, Deanna came to our house. Mother brushed and curled her hair and dressed her in a freshly washed skirt, a starched white blouse, and a pair of snug-fitting shoes. We headed to school with Deanna on one of Dad's arms and me on the other. Admittedly, I was a little jealous of the attention being showered on Deanna—jealous until I saw the joy that flashed across her woebegotten face. I was overcome with childhood tears, and in that moment I understood the difference empathy and compassion can make.

A few days later, I rode my bike to Deanna's house only to find the door locked and the windows shuttered. Emptiness and pain filled my heart, for she, like the other vagabond children, was gone—gone in an instant.

The years, like my childhood, have likewise come and gone. As they passed, I frequently thought of Deanna, but I never saw or heard from her again—not until the day of Mother's funeral.

After the service a vaguely familiar woman with two small children approached me. "I'm sorry for your loss," she began, choking back some tears. I'm not sure you'll remember me. My name's Deanna."

"Of course! I remember you!" I exclaimed. "How wonderful to see you after all this time. How kind of you to come. But how did you know of Mother's passing?"

"I saw her obituary in the newspaper and knew I must come and honor her and your family. Were it not for your mother's kindness and generosity," she continued, "I surely would've starved. Were it not for your father, I would never have known what a kind, patient man looked like. Were it not for you, I would never have known what friendship and belonging looked like."

We sat on a bench outside the funeral home for quite some time, catching up and reminiscing about those childhood days spent playing together. Imagine my surprise when she told me, "I'm happily married to a kind and generous man. We serve as foster parents, giving abandoned and wayward children kindness, respect, and a temporary sense of home and belonging. The two children here with me are two of four children we adopted last year, rescuing them from an abusive father much like my own. I do so wish I'd told your parents the difference they made in one girl's life and continue to make through me in the lives of other forgotten and neglected children. I hope they knew their empathetic hearts and acts of kindness were like little candles, each one lighting countless other candles."

"Not to worry," I smiled and hugged her. "Wherever they are, they know."

We exchanged phone numbers and parted ways, promising to stay in touch. I drove home, the sting of grief over Mother's passing diminished somewhat. I took solace in knowing mother's empathetic nature, her compassionate heart, and her simple acts of kindness were seeds of faith—seeds that took root and spread in all directions. Those roots sprang up and made new trees that in turn sent out roots, and there was indeed no end to the impact both she and my father had.

Deanna's life reminded me that every empathetic heart, every compassionate act no matter how small, has a trickle-down effect, helping the world at large in unforeseen and countless ways. In our complex world, with as many perspectives as there are people, empathy is a powerful force of great emotive value, requiring us to understand

and respond to the suffering of others. Former President Obama has summarized it this way: "Empathy is a quality of character that can change the world—one that makes you understand that your obligations to others extend beyond people who look like you and act like you and live in your neighborhood…and," he continued, "in the words of Dr. Martin Luther King, we are all tied together in a single garment of destiny."

And it is empathy, that uniquely human but powerful force, that binds us together.

Your Reputation Ain't Ruined, Honey
B. Lynn Goodwin

You're a young lady of fifteen, and I'm glad you came to me. Your reputation ain't ruined honey. You have options. If that creep won't marry you, you ain't stuck. Plenty of single women raise babies. Accordin' to the news, some of them even adopt babies. Nobody's gonna shun you. And nobody's gonna say you're easy unless you let 'em. You made a mistake. It's that simple. Gramma and I still love you, and so do your parents. You've just gotta tell 'em. I'll come with you if it'll help. They ain't perfect either. The important thing is that they love you. They want you in their lives. They want you to be happy.

So forget the creep, unless you really love him.

Wait a minute. I know that look.

I ain't even asked. Do ya?

'Cause if you do, that's a whole different story. I can go talk to him if you want. Let him know you have plenty of family. We love you and we ain't gonna let you or this child starve.

The Power of Empathy
Patricia Roop Hollinger

"People with mental illness are not good Christians." Yes, I heard this from the pulpit of my church, while on a weekend pass from the mental hospital where I was receiving psychotherapy and electroshock therapy to treat my descent into Major Depression. I knew what the topic of my next session with my therapist would be. For, you see, I was already dealing with the myriad questions I had regarding religious beliefs that I could not embrace, but then also, fearful of not embracing them.

I was determined to come through this, and one day I heard my "still small voice" (no, I never had auditory hallucinations) tell me, "Some day you will return, but not as a patient."

Upon my release I resumed my college education, which had been so abruptly interrupted. I was also recovering from the loss of my college sweetheart, who ended our relationship when I was hospitalized. At the time I was devastated. However, I now understand how traumatic my illness must have been for him; thus his need to move on with his life.

I was approaching the age of 22. I desperately wanted to be a mother. My younger sister's girlfriend had a brother who was looking for a mate. We were introduced. He was handsome enough. And he was not shocked that I had lost my virginity. His father, being a minister, fulfilled my religious requirements for a mate. I accepted his proposal even though not head-over-heels in love. I had been taught that love hormones were often not to be trusted when looking for a mate.

We married on April 1, 1961. Might that date have been a warning of what lay ahead? I became pregnant when he was told that a child would keep him from being drafted for the Vietnam war. I took to motherhood like a duck takes to water, for my own mother was the textbook example of how to be a good mother. Two years later, I gave birth to our second child. He challenged all my mother skills, as he was born with multiple birth defects, which led to endless screaming and seizures. The most difficult thing I ever did in my life was to seek help in caring for him. His pediatrician's advice led to a hospital that took care of children with such birth defects.

Our family never recovered, since my husband did not fully accept this child's birth. When beautiful women danced on TV, he said aloud, "I wonder if any of them could have normal children?" I never got over that statement, and he never went with me when I visited this child. My energies now focused on our oldest son, whose care often took a back seat when I was attending to his brother. In fact, it was his statement, "Mom, he only has a pain," after I shook his little brother in frustration during a seizure, that led me to seek another care option.

Our life revolved around our employment with Church World Service and attending the Church of the Brethren with other couples our age. It soon became apparent to me that my husband's interest in the wife of one of the couples was more than platonic. Her husband had the same inkling. We confronted them, and yes, they were involved romantically. She made it clear they had plans to be married AND her plan was to gain custody of our healthy son because I had been treated for Major Depression. That is when I wanted to scratch her eyes out, but my pacifist upbringing kicked in and I restrained myself. She might get my husband, but NOT my child.

Even though divorce was right up there with the unpardonable sins, I filed for one. I would deal with the sin part later. During a 10-year hiatus, I figured if robbers and murderers could be forgiven, I could be as well, if I ever chose to remarry.

Then, desperate for some social activity, I attended a Halloween party for singles. One gentleman arrived late, waving a recent warning from a police officer for his speeding. He told the policeman he could not be speeding because the right-side door of his car was not rattling, which it only did when he was speeding. Hey! It was Halloween. The officer gave him a warning just to get away from this man. I was impressed, because the palms of my hands became sweaty, and my heart began to pound, when approached by a police officer. I wanted to take lessons from this man.

At the same time, I had resumed my aborted college education. I made it clear to this man that he would not deter me from completing my education. He not only agreed, he challenged me to complete a master's degree as well. He was in. I completed a B.S. in Social Work, M.S. in Pastoral Counseling, plus the needed credits to become a Licensed Clinical Professional Counselor in the state of Maryland. I was also ordained to ministry in the Church of the Brethren.

During those pursuits, I also joined the Health and Welfare Committee sponsored by the Church of the Brethren and Mennonites, who were exploring ways to inform congregations about the needs of the mentally ill among them. Lo, those many years later, these needs were being openly addressed.

During one of the meetings, the CEO of the hospital where I had been hospitalized during college, passed me a note across the table at a luncheon. It said, "Would you like a job at Brook Lane?" I was aghast! I then recalled the still small voice saying, "Someday you will return, but not as a patient."

Without hesitation, I accepted that offer. I served in the role of Chaplain, Pastoral Counselor, and Licensed Clinical Professional Counselor at Brook Lane for 23 years, and I know without a doubt that I ultimately fulfilled my mission in this lifetime. As I met with patients, I not only brought my educational expertise, but also my own lived experience with mental illness, divorce, and the challenge of caring for a child with birth defects. I have no doubt my clients sensed the empathy I brought to each therapy session.

WHAT DO YOU NEED?
Len Leatherwood

How can I love you better
What is it that you need
How can I help nurture your soul
So your true self can be freed

Tell me the truth
Don't be afraid
Loving means asking
So your joy can pervade

Your true spirit is gliding
Across the sky with ease
Dipping and cavorting
Bolstered by the breeze

How can I love you better
What routes do you wish to explore
How can I help nourish your soul
So you can flourish and soar

The Bridge to Understanding
Juliana Lightle

Give me your hands;
We will walk across the bridge to understanding.

Trade each other's shoes and walk;
We will know each other's struggles, pain, happiness.

Share your voice with me;
We will sing songs of unity and joy.

Join my heart with yours;
We will feel our fears and loves.

Give me your hands;
We will walk across the bridge to understanding.

I Will Take You Halfway
Janet Grace Riehl

At the Albuquerque Airport I stepped out of the car, curbside, looking for some sensible way to carry four containers with only two arms. I was toting two small suitcases, a side bag, and the familiar family solution for overflow—a cardboard box. My friend chauffeuring me spotted the carts. The price seemed right—just a quarter. Yippee! I had a quarter. Satisfied that I was all set, my friend cruised on home. Meanwhile, I approached the carts, quarter in hand. It turned out the carts rented for $3.00 each. Customers pay up front and get a quarter back upon the cart's return. Well, come to think of it, that made more sense. A quarter would have been the 1950s price.

A kindly African-American man—the skycap at the United sidewalk counter—stepped my way, saying, "May I help you?" He explained the cart system to me and said, "Let me get my cart. I'll take you on over to Frontier."

My 90-year-old father, bless his heart, would refer to my skycap as a "colored gentleman." He is a gentleman, that part is for sure. With no eye to current politically correct language trends, I would refer to him, talking to a pal, as "a black man." Our phrases are shaped by the eras we grew up in and those are hard to shake. In my lifespan, I've seen our references move from "Negro," to "Afro-American," to "Black," and back to "African-American."

My new friend was middle-aged, hailed from Detroit, Michigan, and had lived in Albuquerque for over forty years. The Southwest was home now. But his voice had the rich cadence heard in a black Baptist church. I could hear this voice as it rises up singing, as he spoke.

"Your voice does me a world of good," I told my gentleman porter, feeling we were strolling through a railway station in times gone by, feeling as if we were so many places, all at once. "I cannot begin to tell you. It's like hearing good news from home." And it was. His voice went straight inside me.

We entered the door and he smiled, saying, "You just made my day." That's all we said or needed to say. We'd connected, and that's enough. That's a good thing—two human beings connecting. We were not just a black man hustling for the last tip of his shift, or just a white, middle-aged woman with too many bags to carry herself. At the counter he took care of me like a concerned relative; I opened my purse and found a few dollars to press into his hand, while thanking him.

"It's been a pleasure serving you," he offered.

"And it's been a pleasure being served," I replied.

In this brief exchange, we were enacting the ancient call and response of all African languages I've ever encountered. In Twi, the language of the Ashanti tribe in Ghana, West Africa, the leave-taking exchange literally rendered is: "I lay at your feet." With the reply of, "There is no need for you to lay there." It is a way of saying, "I am at your service," which is, I have noticed, a value dying in our own culture.

This exchange between the skycap and myself spanned perhaps ten minutes, yet it made my day, too. The courtesy, graciousness, classiness, intelligence, and rich voice of the man whom I did not exchange names with, had connected me back to a dusty roadside in Ghana, waiting for a small bus, which ran on no particular schedule, to take me to the next village.

Two young women had come with me to help carry my too-heavy bags and then stay with me. They would keep me company until my uncertain transport came and I was safely on it and safely off. This was a scene I'd repeatedly experience throughout the Africa of the 1970s—wherever I went, West, East, or South.

In Botswana, this is the custom of "taking half-way." *(Ke tla boledisa—[kay-kla-bolaydisa]—I will take you halfway)*. In a village one can spend the better part of the day faithfully performing this custom. It works like this. Upon the end of our visit, I escort you at least to the edge of my compound—to its entrance, where the space of my home meets the communal space. We travel the equivalent distance from a Mayberry front door, across the porch, to the sidewalk gate. This African custom is the same as the one in many small towns of seeing off one's guest.

If I have time, I'll continue walking with you across the village, in the direction of your compound. Possibly, we may even hold each other's hands, swinging them happily between us as we chat, until we reach some invisibly intuited point, at which we both understand we must part. Now our call and response ritual begins and goes like this:

Tsamaya Tsincle (Travel/go well), I will tell you, and you will respond, *Tsala Tsintle*. Stay well. And I do. I stay well on the path as you turn, take your first steps toward home, now traveling alone, not in company, with no one to protect you. And I, for my part, breathe in and out the perfume of your presence, turn, and make my way, now alone, not in company, with no one to protect me—towards home.

Thank you, dear-man-who-came-from Michigan-and-talks-with-the-good-news-voice-from-home. Thank you. That is where you took me when you carried my three bags and a box on your railroad porter's cart at the Albuquerque Airport.

I Am Called
Catherine N. Steinberg

I am called into being
with each heart string
that is plucked by another
in need of my compassion.

I am called into being
when all living creatures
seek assistance and refuge
to live freely and unharmed.

I am called into being
when earth, air, fire, and water
need my protection and care
to maintain integrity and balance.

I am called into being
when youth need an elder to listen and
speak to their worries and aspirations
of becoming and bringing their gifts to the world.

I am called into being
when a spirit cries out
in the night needing comfort
from someone who still lives.

I am called into being
with each creative act
that comes from within
reflecting my true essence.

I am called into being
until I am no longer needed
on this physical plane
and my soul is called home.

An Angel with No Wings
Jo Virgil

Not all angels have wings, nor are they literally from heaven. But an angel is someone who knows how to touch your heart and share comfort in a way that truly matters. That was how I got to know Aura. She was there when I needed her, and she helped weave me through a tough time in ways I never imagined I could do.

My husband and I had just gotten home from a trip to Maui to celebrate our 33rd Wedding Anniversary. We had such a close, loving relationship (I thought) and our connection was a treasure to us both (I thought). Then, just three days after we returned from our trip, I came home from work to find a note that he had left me, telling me that he had moved out of the house and filed for divorce. At first, I wondered if that was a joke, but it didn't sound like one my husband would do. And it turned out it wasn't a joke; it was true. He did file for divorce, only telling me that he just wasn't happy—no other explanation. Of course, I never saw that coming, and neither did any of our friends or family. It truly broke my heart.

At the time, though, I was working as Community Relations Manager at Barnes & Noble, and a few days later I had a book group meeting at the store. I needed to be there to lead it. Aura was a member of that group, so I knew her, but not as well as I was about to. At the book discussion, I kept my ordinary professional demeanor; I didn't want to share my hurt with the group and bring them down. But apparently Aura picked up on my inner self. After the book discussion, everyone left and I was on the way to my office. Aura came over to me, gently grabbed my arm, and asked, "What's wrong?"

I wasn't sure I wanted to answer her in a truthful way, but looking into Aura's eyes, I knew that she had a deep insight and a deep compassion. I teared up a bit and then told her the story about my husband leaving me. She tenderly listened, never losing eye contact with me. At the end of my story, she gently smiled and said, "Go get your purse and let's go to lunch. The same thing happened to me, and I survived. So will you."

And that was the beginning of a friendship I had never felt so connected to in my life. Aura knew exactly how to gently guide me through the tough path, always assuring me that I was loved and that my life had meaning. Aura was truly an angel—but not in the way many people imagine! Aura was Jewish from birth, but she didn't believe in a literal God or Heaven; she just knew that kindness and compassion are what matter in life. And she practiced that through every step of her life in ways that truly made a difference. She and I got together often and had conversations that not only helped me heal, but also helped us share stories, laughter, hugs, and genuine truth with each other. Aura was the same age as my mother, who had died a few years before, and she also had a daughter about my age whose name was Jo, the same as mine! Apparently we were meant to be connected.

Aura encouraged me to find my own ways to navigate through this next step of my life, and one idea I came up with made her smile. As the date of my wedding anniversary came up the next year, I decided to have what I called my First Non-Anniversary Party. I invited all my friends and family to come, and asked each of them to bring a story, a photo, or some memorabilia about someone they love, *other than a spouse*. That was to remind me, as Aura always had, that there are lots of different kinds of love in this life, and they all matter. The party was so touching, and it lifted me up into a new kind of comfort in life. Of course Aura was there, and her story to share was about our friendship.

Aura truly was my angel with no wings, and the world around her was truly heaven. She died several years ago, but she lives on in my heart forever. I hope that I learned to pass along the deep compassion she shared with me.

Understood
Jude Walsh

For months, shame, humiliation and fear were my constant companions. I'd found a letter my husband wrote to another woman, begging her to take him back and offering to "lose his family" if only he could be with her. The first thing I did upon finding that letter was throw up. The next thing was to feel deep, visceral fear. My thought was he would take everything, and I would be left with nothing. I would be alone and penniless. I actually counted to see how many tampons I had in case I had no money to buy more. Those were not rational thoughts, but extreme and sudden trauma affects your brain. I was living with a stranger.

We had celebrated our 30th wedding anniversary just weeks before. He wrote in my card, "I have loved you for thirty years and I will love you for many more." He bought me an infinity bracelet, an unending solid gold loop. He made a point to tell me he saw it in a catalog while on a flight and knew it was the perfect anniversary gift for me. This was all so like him. We were high school sweethearts and remained devoted to one another through college, law school, his career climb, and dealing with the complicated health and developmental problems of our much-loved son. He was at the top of his game professionally, litigating an international case. I could finally focus on my career and had teamed up with an amazing group of creative educators. We founded a school that was featured on the front page of *Education Weekly*.

He and I could take a breath and enjoy all we had worked for. Our son's health had improved, so we felt it was safe to travel internationally. We enjoyed a walking trip in Provence, a sailboat cruise in the Adriatic, and a wonderful trip to England. At the end of the England trip, after being together 24/7 for a week, he went to the post office to mail home some souvenirs. When he returned, he hugged me and said, "Can you believe it? I missed you while I was gone." So sweet. I was grateful for everything. Life was good.

Then he began acting a bit erratically, being short with me and our son, and critical of everything and anything I did. Nothing seemed to please him, not even his work. I thought he might be having a midlife crisis and just vowed to be patient and love him through it. He was so not himself though, that I finally did something I had never done before. I went through his briefcase. I was concerned that something was wrong at work. That's when I found the letter.

How could this be? How could this man, the man I trusted above all others and loved with every fiber of my being, be having an affair? Worse, be willing to ditch his family if she would take him back. Clearly, this had been going on for a while and she had ended it. He was grieving the "most profound loss" of her. Not only was I traumatized, but I was also humiliated. I was proud of our marriage, our family, and our devotion to one another. People often remarked that they wanted to have the marriage we had. What happened?

I kept his betrayal a secret, mostly because I thought he would come to his senses and we would heal, be better than ever. And oddly, I did not want people to think ill of him. When I confronted him, I found out he had been seeing a therapist, another secret, and we met with his therapist the next day. The therapist said my husband had come to him filled with grief and shame and wanting to make things right. He advised him to not tell me and just clean up the mess he had made and do better as a husband and father. That outraged me, leaving me out of the choice entirely. It's interesting that I could be angry with the therapist but not my husband.

We went to therapy once a week for months until I found out he had again been lying to me, was in contact with this other woman the entire time and thought he might want to "go in that direction." Something in me snapped. I knew I had to stop worrying about him and take care of myself and my son. I got my own therapist, a specialist in men and midlife crises, and he was quite blunt with me. My husband's relationship with this other woman would never work out because it was an addiction. But even if it ended, the therapist could not be certain our marriage was salvageable. He strongly suggested I find a COSA group and begin to go. COSA stands for Codependents of Sex Addicts. How had my life come to this? I'm codependent? He's a sex addict? My beautiful perfect marriage to the most wonderful man in the world felt like a sham. I did not trust my own ability to see what was true or possible, but I trusted my therapist. I found a local COSA group and called the contact number.

The sweetest woman answered. She immediately shared some of her story, not so different from mine, and assured me I would be welcome. She stressed that the meetings were a safe place and that anything I heard or said there must be kept confidential. That made me feel a bit better but the very idea of having to go hang out with a bunch of women, at least I assumed they would all be women, whose partners were sex addicts, was discouraging. I had always thought of myself as emotionally strong, resilient even. Now I felt weak, vulnerable, inadequate.

She met me a half-hour before the meeting and went over the rules with me: just first names, no interrupting, and again, confidentiality. The meeting began with a reading of the 12 Steps just like any AA meeting I had seen on TV. The first woman who spoke told of her decision to end her marriage. She'd had enough and it was over. This was NOT what I wanted to hear. I thought all these women would be like me and want to save their marriages. The next few who chose to speak shared what they were struggling with. No one jumped in and said try this or try that. We all just listened. The person chairing asked if anyone else wanted to speak.

To my astonishment, I raised my hand. "My name is Jude, and I am a codependent to a sex addict." I felt relief fill my body just saying those words aloud. My feelings were still raw. I had shared them with so few. Eyes downcast, I told my story. I cried. I choked over certain words and facts. When I was finished, I looked up through my tears. Every single woman had her eyes on me. Every single one leaned in and met my eyes when I looked at her. I saw NO judgment. I saw and felt acceptance. I saw and felt compassion, not pity. For the first time since I read that damn letter, I felt seen. I felt understood.

I met with those women, and others like them, once a week for over ten years. I found that hour-and-a-half each week to be a lifeline. I witnessed the struggle and anguish of women whose lives had been upended, their trust shattered. I learned the power of acceptance. I learned the power of speaking the truth even when the truth hurts. I learned to trust myself again. And I learned how to be present for others. To witness their struggle and pain and just hold it, not try to fix it. To see them and understand. To be seen and understood. And that is everything.

How To Save Your Life
Linda C. Wisniewski

(After Lorrie Moore's short story, "How to Be a Writer")

1. Tell your best friend you're tired of being cooped up in your house with your fiscally conservative/socially liberal husband for 2,982 days, 14 hours and 22 minutes, give or take a half-hour here and there, as the world deals with a global pandemic.
2. Listen without interrupting as you usually do while your friend complains about her musician husband's incessant ukulele practice day after bloody day.
3. Devote the next three days to comparing the length of your conversations. Did she let you talk as long as you let her?
4. Set aside time each morning to search for news stories online about vaccine availability in your area.

5. Read for hours uncounted, because who cares what time it is or how much time you spend online for more news about the botched rollout of vaccines and who is to blame for that.
6. Discover your place in the population of humans eligible for the vaccine. What stage in your state do you fall in?
7. Detour for an hour or two when you see interesting or alarming or upsetting news online.
8. Over lunch each day, turn on the small TV in your kitchen and get indigestion as you eat a sandwich and watch CNN or MSNBC reporting on the pandemic. For a change, watch the local channels for news about the increased shootings in the nearby city.
9. Discover you are in Group 1C, for people over 65 but after all healthcare workers, first responders, and essential workers, and those residing in nursing homes.
10. Wish for only the second time in your life that you were just a little bit older.
11. Remember the first time, waiting outside a bar on a Friday night with your high school friends while the one who is 18 goes inside to buy a six-pack he has promised to share.
12. Wish you were 17 again and there was no pandemic, and you were fresh and young and your only care in the world was whether you'd all get caught drinking underage.
13. Read a text message from your son in New York City: "You can get vaccinated in NYC starting Monday. Over 65!"
14. Feel your hands sweat as you click on the link he sends and read that it is for New Yorkers, which you have not been since 1969.
15. You feel yourself becoming desperate. You have been good, wearing a mask, staying home. You deserve this vaccine now.
16. You contemplate Googling "how to make a fake ID." You know this search will be in your computer's history forever and then floating somewhere in the "cloud," but so what? Will they throw an elderly white lady with no priors in jail? Doubtful.
17. You think of changing the state on your driver's license. But you see it has a shadow underneath with an American flag on the front and Pennsylvania 1787 on the back.
18. You go online and Google "how to make a fake ID." You click on the one for ID Warehouse and follow the instructions. You must

order special paper, hologram overlays, and some other stuff, but thank you, Amazon Prime, they are on your doorstep the next day.
19. When your new Fake NYS ID is as perfect as you can make it, you click on the NYS official website and, using your 1964 New York address, you schedule an appointment for the next Monday afternoon.
20. On Sunday evening, you lay out your clothes for the next day. You contact your son in Brooklyn and tell him what you are about to do. "Good luck," he texts.
21. Monday morning, you eat a bowl of Cheerios, take a shower and blow dry your hair. You dress conservatively, in black slacks, a quilted black jacket and high black boots. You will fit right in.
22. You drive across the river into New Jersey. Traffic is light, and you realize most people are working from home or staying home. You notice the huge parking lot at the Paramus Shopping Center is half empty. You're not sure if that's good (people are being safe) or bad (people are afraid to go shopping).
23. You enter the squeeze of cars approaching the Holland Tunnel. This, at least, feels normal. When you come out at the other end, the sunlight blinds you for a second and you pull down your visor. The female voice on your GPS guides you to the mass vaccination clinic at the Javits Center. You thank her out loud because nobody can hear and she's not so annoying today.
24. You pull into a parking lot on Tenth Avenue and hand your keys to the valet. You hop out and walk a block west on your shiny black boots. Soon you will be protected from this nightmarish virus, and all because you are so smart.
25. It's cold, so you step up your pace until you reach the big glass doors. You pull the long metal handle and let yourself inside the building. You pull your mask from your pocket and put it on. Hordes of other masked people mill around, looking for where to go. Uniformed guards point you all down a hall to your left, and you follow, trying to maintain a social distance of six feet.
26. An older woman, in other words, a woman your age, cries out loudly in a foreign language you don't recognize. A teenaged girl tries to comfort her as she rummages through a large cloth bag.
27. The girl looks around the cavernous room, then down at the floor all around them. She walks away from the older lady, scanning the ground with her eyes. Shaking her head, she slow walks back to the wall where the woman wails.

28. You ask if you can help. The teen tells you the woman has lost her ID. She cannot get vaccinated without it, and she is a grandmother raising three grandchildren alone. She cleans rooms in a hotel and is afraid of catching the virus, but she has to go to work. She has to, the girl says, near tears herself.
29. You take a deep slow breath. You walk away, toward the huge windows. You look outside at the sunlit empty street.
30. You reach inside your handbag and pull out the New York State ID you carefully crafted. The older woman has stopped crying and stares at you warily. The teenager puts an arm around her. You give the girl your ID.
31. You tell her your appointment is at three, and her grandmother can have it. The teen's mouth falls open. Go ahead, you say, she needs it more than I do.
32. The teenager pulls her grandmother away from the wall, thanks you, and scurries down the hall.
33. One of the guards walks up and asks if you need help. You tell him no, and ask him how long it takes to get the vaccine.
34. He says once you're inside, about an hour. You thank the guard for his help.
35. Outside, you walk north, feeling the sun on your shoulders. The occasional beep of a truck backing up or an impatient taxi horn recalls for you the old New York, last year, before the virus. Walk and walk, breathing deeply through your mask, making eye contact with people you pass, their eyes visible about the cloth covering their mouths and noses. Nod to see them nod back at you.
36. Some of them may be infected with COVID. Maybe they don't even know it. Maybe you are too. This should scare you. But not today. Today you feel one with them, a small drop in the moving tide.
37. Do you want to know the rest of this story? Walk back to the place where you started and wait on the sidewalk. Soon the old woman and her grandchild will step out into the sunshine. They will raise their folded hands to the sky. Wipe tears from your eyes and go home.

Previously published in slightly altered form, *Pearl S. Buck Writing Center Literary Magazine*, Winter 2020. https://psbwritingcenter.org/page/3/

I Live In A Boy's Body
Margie Witt

I live in a boy's body.

My junior high classmates discover my secret and what begins as trivial insults directed at my femininity escalates to painful bullying.

At night, I fire up my computer intending to tackle my homework. Instead, I disappear into the video game that plays across my screen. I find myself shooting down the enemies. I am confused. I can't concentrate on my assignments and I begin to fail. The school administrators send me to the classroom where special children are educated. I am one of them now. More fuel for the bullies.

Teachers send me to the office when I arrive on campus in a long black raincoat on a sunny day. It's the anniversary of the Columbine shooting and they are all on guard. I am sent home and hours later my mom answers a persistent knock at the door to find two police officers. I convince them it was all a dare from an online friend. I am accused of bullying. They can't see who I am.

I begin to plan my suicide. One day I whisper the word suicide to another student and the Special Ed aide sends me to the office. The school psychologist questions my motives, which brings on a roller coaster of emotions. Next thing I know I am secured to a hospital bed in a room with a guard outside my door. A doctor asks the usual questions and I shake my head in response. No, I don't do drugs. No, I don't starve myself or vomit after binges of food. Even she can't see why I am there. She writes on my chart "Suicidal ideation" and sends me off with the guard to the psychiatric unit. Because of one suicidal comment they must hold me for 72 hours.

I'm stripped down and given a thin white t-shirt, sweatpants and laceless shoes. The room I share has two cots, two plastic chairs, and no mirrors. A bright fluorescent light controlled by a switch outside our locked door illuminates the room. My roommate and I lay on our cots staring at the ceiling. "What're you in for?" he asks, turning towards me. That's when he notices my breasts beneath the thin white shirt and the bullying begins. He could see who I am.

Three days later, I return home to a room that has been meticulously cleaned. My belongings are stacked in the closet in clear plastic storage bins, everything visible. No place to hide anything. My karate weapons have been confiscated but my *gi* hangs prominently above a rainbow display of belts. Even my sensei hadn't noticed I am different.

The world goes on a lockdown as a mysterious virus rampages around the globe. My parents are glued to the TV and don't seem to notice that I never come out of my room. A two-week stay-at-home order turns into a month, then a year. Persistent messages from school about missed assignments go unheeded. For once, I am not unique. Most students of the class of 2021 are doing the same, staying in their room, stuck in the midst of this pandemic.

I look for friends like me online and gather my resources, finally building up the confidence to leave the comfort of my room. I catch my mom staring at my long black nails. Her eyes roll past my blooming breasts, and for a moment she gazes into my made-up eyes. She touches my shoulder length hair. "I could trim that for you," she offers.

"Don't you see?" I ask. She sits in startled silence for a moment, stands up, and leaves the room. *She still doesn't know who I am,* I think.

She returns with a small pink cosmetic bag and a manicure kit. With a tender touch, she reaches for my hand and dabs at my nails with a moistened soft cotton ball. "Let's see what we can do about those chipped nails." The next day there's another pink cosmetic bag on my bathroom counter. This one has a glorious assortment of lipsticks.

What's your story? It's all in the telling.
Stories are compasses and architecture;
we navigate by them,
we build our sanctuaries and our prisons out of them,
and to be without a story is to be
lost in the vastness of a world that
spreads in all directions like arctic tundra or sea ice.
To love someone is to put yourself in their place,
we say, which is to put yourself in their story,
or figure out how to tell yourself their story.
Which means that a place is a story,
and stories are geography,
and empathy is first of all an
act of imagination, a storyteller's art,
and then a way of traveling from here to there.

— Rebecca Solnit

Books Published by Story Circle Network

Inside and Out: Women's Truths, Women's Stories
edited by Susan F. Schoch

Kitchen Table Stories
edited by Jane Ross

Starting Points
by Susan Wittig Albert

True Words from Real Women, the SCN Anthology, 2009-2014
edited by Amber Lea Starfire, Mary Jo Doig, Susan F. Schoch

Real Women Write: Sharing Our Stories, Sharing Our Lives,
the SCN Anthology, 2015-2019
edited by Susan F. Schoch

What Wildness Is This: Women Write About the Southwest
edited by Susan Wittig Albert, Susan Hanson,
Jan Epton Seale, Paula Stallings Yost

*With Courage and Common Sense:
Memoirs from the Older Women's Legacy Circle*
edited by Susan Wittig Albert and Dayna Finet

Writing From Life
by Susan Wittig Albert

"Sometimes it's not the book.
It's where the reader is on her journey."

— Susan Wittig Albert

This book was designed using
Proxima Nova, Eccentric, and Adobe Garamond.
Designed and typeset by Sherry Wachter:
sherry@sherrywachter.com

Made in the USA
Middletown, DE
02 February 2023